ISBN: 9798322732082

Imprint: Independently published
www.truecrimeuk.co.uk

Table of Contents

Unsolved 1962

- Ben Ward
- Mabel Metcalfe
- Dolores Garcia Vasquez
- Newly Born Female Child
- Robert Allen
- Annie Mary ODonnell
- James Albert Kenyon
- Joseph McEwan
- Dennis Hurley
- Augustine P Dooley
- Baby
- New Born Girl
- Wesley Spencer McCallum
- Geffrey Bacon
- Robert Jenkins
- Olive Mary Duncan
- John McDonald
- Baby
- George Bailey
- John McGourty
- Baby
- Baby
- Baby
- Michael James Reynolds
- Laurel Barrett
- Winifred Williams
- Jacqueline Boyle
- Bertha Davies
- William Johnstone
- Purnesh Chandra Paul
- Billy Holloway
- Joseph Augustus Hedley
- Susan Michelmore
- Alan John Vigar
- Norman Rickard

- Lily Stephenson
- Bryan Jackson and Noel Mellors
- New Born Boy
- William Anthony Hamilton
- Joseph Maguire
- Edward Hunter
- Agnes Walsh
- John Brown
- John McNally

Unsolved 1962

A list of unsolved cases for 1962.

Ben Ward

Age: unknown

Sex: male

Date: 31 Dec 1962

Place: Wynford Road, Islington, London

Ben Ward was found battered to death in his shed on a building site in Wynford Road, Islington on the night of 31 December 1962.

It was thought that he might have been murdered 'for kicks' by a New Year's reveller.

It was thought that he had been struck from behind as he sat in his swivel chair. The murder weapon had been a scarifier, a metal instrument used in the building trade which weighed at least 20lb.

Footprints were found in the snow circling the shed that were made by a man wearing square-toed shoes and photographs of them were taken by the police.

It was said that there was no sign of a struggle, and that nothing was missing and Ben Ward had not been robbed.

The last person to have seen him alive was a timekeeper on the site. He said, 'I saw Ben at 4.40pm on Monday. As I left the site he called 'cheerio, a happy New Year'.

The police carried out a reconstruction of the murder and said that they were certain that his killer had been a tall man of great strength, noting that it appeared that he had wielded the scarifier with one hand, striking Ben Ward with it several times.

Ben Ward had lived in Allison Road, Hornsey.

Mabel Metcalfe

Age: 73

Sex: female

Date: 17 Nov 1962

Place: Springfield House, Halifax Road, Dewsbury

Mabel Metcalfe was found dead on a footpath near her home at Springfield House in Dewsbury on 17 November 1962.

Her body was found by a postman and it was thought that she had been dead for some hours.

She had been a secretary at a firm of rag merchants.

The police said that they were considering whether the murder was connected to that of Lily Stephenson at Barnsley on 31 January 1962. They said that on the surface they appeared to be very similar. It was noted that Dewsbury and Barnsley were 16 miles apart. Lily Stephenson had been hit in the face and raped. However, it was heard that she had been extremely ill and that her injuries would not have killed a normally healthy person.

The police said that they were treating Mabel Metcalfe's death as a murder, but that they would not be disclosing the cause of death, or say whether she had been attacked or whether anything had been missing.

Mabel Metcalfe had lived alone.

She was last seen near Dewsbury bus station at about 11pm on the Friday and the police appealed for anyone who saw her after that to come forward.

Dolores Garcia Vasquez

Age: 30

Sex: female

Date: 16 Nov 1962

Place: Radnor Walk, Chelsea, London

Dolores Garcia Vasquez died from an abortion.

However, it was not possible to say whether it was self-induced or had been brought about by some other person.

She had been a domestic servant at a property in Radnor Walk, Chelsea where she had worked for the previous 16 months.

An open verdict was returned at her inquest, with the Coroner stating that there was insufficient evidence as to the circumstances.

She was admitted to St George's Hospital on 16 November 1962 after complaining of severe abdominal pains and was found to be 20 week's pregnant, however, the hospital were unable to diagnose the exact trouble. She was found to have had some signs of an infection and was treated for that but she died 2½ hours later.

She had denied any interference by instrument.

The doctor that carried out her post mortem gave her cause of death as peritonitis due to septic abortion.

It was heard that the presence of some infection did suggest that interference took place, and that that was a strong possibility, but there was no direct evidence.

A police detective said that he had made exhaustive inquiries as to whether or not there had been a self-induced abortion or one caused by some other person, but had been unable to find out.

An open verdict was returned.

Newly Born Female Child

Age: 0

Sex: female

Date: 12 Nov 1962

Place: London

A newly born female child was reported to have been found murdered by the Metropolitan Police in their Homicide Returns for 1962.

However, no further developments are known.

In their return they stated:

Efforts to trace the parents have not been successful. This crime remains unsolved at 30th April 1963.

Robert Allen

Age: 70

Sex: male

Date: 28 Oct 1962

Place: The Hut, Hitchin Road, Pegsden, Bedfordshire.

Robert Allen died after being physically assaulted in Pegsden on the night of 20-21 October 1962.

He later died in hospital on 28 October 1962.

The prosecution dropped a charge against three men due to lack of evidence.

A verdict of murder by a person or persons unknown was later recorded at the inquest in St Pancras on Thursday 3 January 1963.

Robert Allen had lived in The Hut, also known as the Cabin, in Hitchin Road in Pegsden and was assaulted there by several people and subsequently died from his injuries seven days later.

The landlord of the Live and Let Live public house in Pegsden said that Robert Allen left his house at closing time on the Saturday night, 20 October 1962 and that when he called to see him the following morning that he found him in a chair 'in a terrible state, hardly recognisable. Everything was in disorder'.

A woman that could see the hut from her window said that at about midnight on 20 October 1962 that she heard voices arguing for about 20 minutes.

The pathologist that carried out the post mortem examination said that Robert Allen died from head injuries consistent with blows to the face, and possibly from a shod foot.

A press operator that lived in Long Road, Pegsdon, said that Robert Allen kept pigs and that he had sold four in the two or three weeks before his murder. He said that he spoke to him on the Friday night and that he had spoken of a subsidy and showed him a cheque for about £14. He added:

I went round to see him the next morning and saw the place upside down. A transistor radio was missing.

A police inspector said that more money was found in the shack than Robert Allen would have received for the pigs.

Although no trial was held, the Homicide Return for 1962 for the Bedfordshire Constabulary named four people that they strongly suspected of having committing the murder. They were all dealers or gypsies, detailed:

1. Male, aged 19.
2. Male, aged 22.
3. Male, aged 43.
4. Male, aged 39.

The details in the 1962 Homicide Return from Bedfordshire constabulary stated:

The four suspects named at 2 above are strongly suspected of committing this murder. The file of papers has been submitted to the Director of Prosecutions who on 25th April, 1963, informed me that in his view the enquiries do not, at this stage, disclose sufficient evidence to justify proceedings on a charge of murder against anyone.

In addition to the property alleged to have been stolen (mentioned on part I of the return) it is believed that a sum of money may have also been stolen. The four suspects were known to the victim and were camping in the neighbourhood during the material times. The motive for the murder, although not established beyond doubt, appears to have been theft. The four suspects are thought to have punched and possibly kicked and assaulted the victim with a beer bottle.

The details for the case are held at the National Archives at Kew in file DPP 2/3568, but it is closed until 2044.

Annie Mary ODonnell

Age: 73

Sex: female

Date: 12 Oct 1962

Place: 32 Victoria Dwellings, Clerkenwell Road, Clerkenwell, London

Annie Mary O'Donnell was killed in her religious bookshop at 32 Victoria Dwellings, Clerkenwell Road in Clerkenwell, London on 12 October 1962.

An 18-year-old butcher was tried three times for her murder but acquitted.

The jury failed to reach a verdict at the first two trials and the prosecution presented no evidence at the third. The dates of the trials at the Old Bailey were:

1. 12 February 1963.
2. 7 March 1963.
3. 8 March 1963.

However, it was noted that following the release of the butcher he assaulted a woman in Petty France, Westminster, with intent to rob her on 3 May 1963, for which he was convicted on 29 May 1963.

Victoria Dwellings has since been demolished and the plot redeveloped, however, Herbal Hill and Clerkenwell

Road are still there along with many other period buildings.

Background and Habits of Annie O'Donnell

Annie O'Donnell had been a single woman, born in Clonmel, Eire on 4 December 1887, however, the police were unable to trace any blood relatives.

Although she was 74 years of age, she was described as a well preserved woman in good health.

She had been a staunch Roman Catholic and attended church twice a day, living an insular life and having no close friends, her acquaintances all being people concerned in her religious activities.

She had lived in a single-roomed flat at 39 Coldbath Buildings in Rosebery Avenue, WC1, but the greater part of her day was spent at her shop, the Catholic Repository at 32 Victoria Dwellings at the corner of Clerkenwell Road and Herbal Hill where she sold a miscellaneous assortment of articles, all to do with the Roman Catholic faith, such as statues, crucifixes, rosaries, holy medals, prayer books, religious cards and calendars.

The police report stated that it was difficult to assess the volume of her business carried on at the shop, but noted that it had been variously described as 'quiet' and 'busy'.

However, it was noted that Annie O'Donnell was a person of some substance, it being found that at the time of her death she had had a belt containing £599 sewn into her underskirt.

The nearest person traced to her was her god-daughter who lived at 5 Cave Road, E13. She said that when she was young that she also lived in Coldbath Buildings after her parents separated and Annie O'Donnell helped her out. She said that it was through Annie O'Donnell's influence that she embraced the Roman Catholic religion.

Location of 32 Victoria Dwellings, Clerkenwell Road today

She said that she visited Annie O'Donnell regularly, but that the last time she saw her was on Sunday 7 October 1962.

Annie O'Donnell's god-daughter confirmed that Annie O'Donnell had been a very quiet person, with no friends, who spent almost her entire day either in her shop or in St Peter's Church nearby in Clerkenwell Road. She added that church and her religion were her sole topics of conversation, and that she didn't disclose her financial status with her but that she always had the impression that she was 'comfortably off'.

First Police Officer on the Scene

The first police officer on the scene had known Annie O'Donnell as keeping her shop at 32 Victoria Dwellings for 24 years. It was he and the neighbour at 32 Victoria Dwellings who identified her body.

Neighbour

Annie O'Donnell's neighbour at 33 Victoria Dwellings, opposite 32, knew most about Annie O'Donnell's habits and movements. She described her as very quiet, but that she had little to do with her over the four years that she had lived at the address.

She said that Annie O'Donnell would close her shop between 6pm and 6.30pm and then go up Clerkenwell Road towards St Peter's Church, which was close by and would generally return about 7pm. She said that she thought that Annie O'Donnell would then cook herself a meal before going to the 8pm Mass, also at St Peter's Church. It was noted that by Mass, the neighbour meant the 8pm Benediction Service. The neighbour added that on some occasions Annie O'Donnell would return and stay in the shop until about 9pm.

The neighbour further noted that at about 7.50pm, the bell at St Peter's Church would be run, calling people to the 8pm Benediction Service and that it was usually immediately after that that she would hear Annie O'Donnell locking up and leaving for church. It was additionally noted that the noise of the bell, in the nearby dwellings, was deafening, and obliterated all other sounds.

The neighbour said that it was her recollection that after business hours, that Annie O'Donnell would lock her door from the inside if she was in the shop and would not answer to any knocking. However, it was noted that if the evidence of another neighbour was accepted, then that would not have appeared to have been the case on the evening of the murder.

It was noted that the neighbour at 33 Victoria Dwellings was the last person known to have seen Annie O'Donnell before her murder, that being about 7.10pm or 7.15pm on 12 October 1962.

Father at St Peter's Italian Church

The Father at St Peter's Italian Church in Clerkenwell Road said that he knew Annie O'Donnell extremely well and that to his recollection that she would attend every night for the Evening Benediction at 8pm and that he had never known her to be late and that she would also attend at other times during the day, especially on Friday evenings. He noted that Friday evenings were a particular day of devotion in the Roman Catholic faith and the Father said that it was his belief that Annie O'Donnell would attend at about 6.30pm to 7pm to perform the Stations of the Cross privately.

The Father noted that Annie O'Donnell didn't attend the Benediction on Friday 12 October 1962 and the police said that they were unable to trace anyone who could say that she had attended church earlier that day.

Woman from 11 Griffin Mansions

A woman from 11 Griffin Mansions said it had been Annie O'Donnell's habit to leave her shop for church every evening at about 7.50pm and that she understood her to have money, but had no reason for knowing that apart from local gossip.

Description of Scene

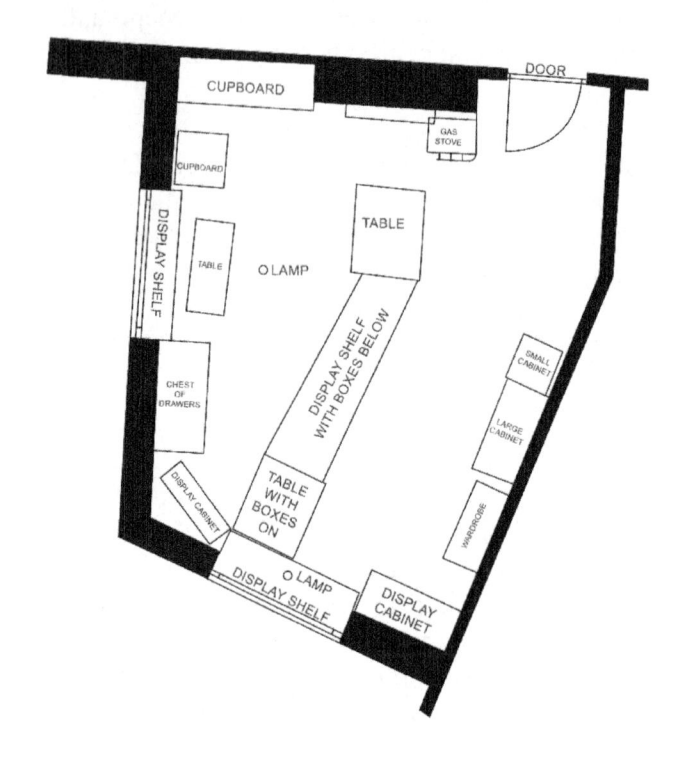

Plan of 32 Victoria Dwellings, Clerkenwell Road

The attack on Annie O'Donnell took place in her shop, which was a single ground floor corner room of a block of flats, 32 Victoria Dwellings, bounded on one side by Clerkenwell Road and on the other by Herbal Hill, plans of which were made for the Court hearing.

There was but one door that opened from a passageway leading from the common entrance to the flats in Herbal Hill. The door was fitted with one mortice type lock, and although other locks had been fitted at one time or another, they were no longer operative.

The door was panelled in wood and an electric light switch was situated just inside the door on the wall. There were two windows, one overlooking Clerkenwell Road and the other the corner of Herbal Hill, both of which were used for display purposes and hung with religious cards and calendars along with a number of religious statues.

The room was noted for being a peculiar shape, the walls being of different lengths:

1. North wall, where door was located: 14ft 7in.
2. East wall: 19ft 6in.
3. South wall: 10ft 8in, (Clerkenwell Road).
4. West wall: 14ft 8½in, (Herbal Hill).

Running for almost the length of the shop, from south to north, there was a counter, 2ft 2in wide, to which had been added a desk which was 3ft long, leaving a space of 2ft 4½in between the end of the desk and the wall. It was noted that the desk had been described in some people's evidence as a 'table'. It was in that space between the end of the table and the wall, near to the gas stove, that Annie O'Donnell usually stood in the shop, and it was on the customer's side of the counter at that point where her body was later found.

The room was illuminated by two naked electric light bulbs, one being above the display window in Clerkenwell Road, and the other hanging from the ceiling approximately over the centre of the counter. However, it was noted that the street lighting was sufficient to light the room to some extent otherwise.

Discovery of the Crime

Annie O'Donnell's body was found by a woman that had lived at 38 Victoria Dwellings and her brother. The woman had left her flat at about 7.45pm to 8pm to visit her brother, a bank messenger, who lived in a different block of the same dwellings, 122 Victoria Dwellings. On her way out she noticed that the door to Annie O'Donnell's shop was ajar, but said that she couldn't say whether there had been any lights on in the room at the time. She later returned home at about 10.30pm with her brother, and noticed that the door was still ajar and that there were no lights on in the room.

She said that she pointed that out to her brother who then pushed the door, but it only opened a little way, after which he switched the light on, the switch being just inside the door, and when he looked in he saw Annie O'Donnell lying on the floor just inside the door, with her feet pointing to the left wall, and her head, which was in a pool of blood, near to the table.

The woman's brother then ran off to the Hat and Tun public house nearby and telephoned for the police, the call being made at 10.30pm.

Meanwhile, a man was called by his wife and he entered the room and felt Annie O'Donnell's wrist and found her to be cold, but still breathing.

The woman's brother by then returned from telephoning the police, and when he entered the room he removed the chair from where it had been behind the door, to where it was when the room was photographed.

The police arrived at 10.45pm and when one of them examined Annie O'Donnell, he heard her gurgle and then immediately went off to telephone for an ambulance.

Before she was taken away by the ambulance, a priest from St Peter's Church nearby and a father gave her absolution.

When the ambulance arrived at St Bartholemew's Hospital, Annie O'Donnell was examined in the ambulance by the medical registrar, who found her to be dead, that being at 11.05pm. He added that he formed the opinion that she had been recently dead.

He said that when he examined her body that he found no obvious disarrangement of the clothing.

Her body was then removed to the mortuary, but upon the insistence of a police constable with the City of London Police, it was removed to the City of London's Coroner's Mortuary in Golden Lane.

Following that, photographs of her body and her room were taken by the police and the room examined for fingerprints.

At 3.30am, the police searched Annie O'Donnell's body and removed an underskirt, in which a strip of canvas in the shape of a belt was securely stitched to the inside front. The belt was in four compartments and it was obvious that it contained bank notes. It was noted that the police decided to wait for the call of a relative before opening the belt, however, as no relative was forthcoming by 4.15pm on 14 October 1962, the belt was opened in the presence of a father, and found to contain £599.

It was noted that no other money was found on her body, nor in the room itself, apart from a tin box that contained 43 shilling pieces and another tin box containing 7/4d in copper.

Post Mortem Examination

The post mortem examination was carried out at 8.30am on 13 October 1962 at the City of London Mortuary in Golden Lane.

The pathologist said that he found injuries to her right lower jaw, left temple, left ear and cheek, which he said he thought were consistent with blows from a flat surfaced blunt instrument, but more suggestive of heavy falls against furniture or the floor and less consistent with blows from a fist. He added that a bruise behind her left shoulder was similarly consistent with a fall.

He said that he also found bruises on the back of her hands and right arm which he said were consistent with Annie O'Donnell trying to protect herself.

He also found split wounds to her scalp, which gave clear evidence of a single, and possibly the first disabling, blow to the front of her head, along with seven others in two areas, delivered at three different angles, possibly when she was no longer standing. He added that those to the back of her head were probably the last to be sustained and added that they were all suggestive of the use of some weapon such as a tyre lever or poker.

He said that he found her skull to be fractured and thrust into the surface of her brain above the right ear and concluded that her cause of death was intercranial haemorrhage due to a fractured skull and lacerated brain.

Following the post mortem examination, the pathologist went to 32 Victoria Dwellings along with the Laboratory Liaison Officer, and it was established that the only blood splashes found were the two series near to the gas stove, giving support to the pathologists observations that certain of the blows were struck when Annie O'Donnell was no longer standing.

Oil painting of 32 Victoria Dwellings, from original police photo

It was considered that the attack on Annie O'Donnell had been confined to the part of the shop that lay behind the door and to the front, or public side, of the counter where there was a large pool of blood congealing. There was little evidence of blood splattering found, but the two signs of it were:

1. Directly on to the paper that was inserted in the bottom of the gas stove.
2. Immediately in front of the gas stove, on the floor, that being consistent with a blow struck whilst Annie O'Donnell's head was near the floor.

There was also bloodstaining at the foot of the table extension of the counter, but that was smeared and consistent to having been caused by involuntary movements of Annie O'Donnell's head whilst she lay on the floor. There was also some lesser staining that was cause by the ambulance men when they placed Annie O'Donnell on the stretcher.

It was noted that the customer's side of the counter had not been disturbed to any great extent. However, the other side of the counter was utter confusion, with a cupboard that was built into the north wall having been opened and ransacked. The drawers to the table had also been pulled out and the contents scattered. It was noted that it was fair to say that the back of the counter was not normally tidy, but that it had never been in the condition that it was found following the murder.

Enquiries At The Scene

Immediately following upon the discovery of the crime, officers, both uniformed and CID, were mustered and an organised search of the vicinity was made which continued for days to follow.

During the search the police received the utmost co-operation from the local authorities, even to the extent of opening sewers and disused drains. However, it was stated that it could not be said with any certainty that the murder weapon had been found, however, a thin cold chisel was found in a wet drain near to the scene which gave a slight reaction to the Benzedine test, the presumptive test for blood, but apart from that, there was no other evidence to connect it to the crime.

On 15 October 1962, whilst undertaking an organised search of the electrified railway lines that ran under Vine Street Bridge, a police detective found a Roman Catholic Identity card and a buff envelope containing a wartime Identity Card, both being in the name of Annie O'Donnell, along with some 1½d postage stamps and a sheet of printed paper. They were all taken to the

Fingerprint Department, but certain prints found were eliminated as being those of the police detective who found them.

Other officers were directed to make a house to house search in the vicinity to trace possible witnesses which disclosed a number of people who could speak of the condition of the door of the shop and the lights during the evening of 12 October 1962, the statements being summarised as:

1. 6.05pm: Man and Woman, left shop leaving an unknown blonde woman there.
2. 6.30pm: Woman, passed shop, door ajar and lights out.
3. 7.00pm: Schoolboy, said door was definitely shut.
4. About 7.00pm: Woman, said lights were on.
5. 7.05pm: Woman, said definitely that the door was closed and the lights were off.
6. 7.10pm to 7.15pm: Woman, saw Annie O'Donnell return to her shop and unlock the door.
7. 7.30pm: Two women, stated that the door had been open.
8. 7.35pm: Woman, said that light was on and shop door was about one foot ajar.
9. 7.40pm: Man, said the door was open.
10. About 7.45pm: Woman, said the lights were off. However, it was stated that she was unreliable and later complicated the issue by saying that the lights were on at 9pm, it being noted that it was significant that she had been visiting public houses between the times she mentioned.
11. 7.50pm: Woman, said the lights were out.
12. 8.00pm to 8.30pm: A Father, said Annie O'Donnell didn't arrive at church.
13. 8.25pm: Man, said lights were out and door closed.
14. 9.00pm: Woman, described as unreliable in her 7.45pm observation, said the lights were on.
15. 10.30pm: Woman and her brother, discover the crime.

It was noted by the police that the only information really out of place was that given by the unreliable woman who said that the lights were on at 9pm.

Woman From 9-10 Victoria Buildings

A 38-year-old woman who had been the tenant of the first floor flats at 9-10 Victoria Buildings said that she had been there for nearly 20 years and had seen the lady in the statue shop on various occasions, but had never spoken or associated with her herself.

She said that on 12 October 1962 she stayed in until 1.40pm when she went to work at Holborn and returned home at about 5.30pm.

She noted that she had never noticed if the shop had been open as she had never had occasion to enter the dwellings.

She said that she then stayed in until 8.15pm at which time she happened to look out of her kitchen window which overlooked the junction of Herbal Hill and Clerkenwell Road, and saw a youth standing in the street looking nervous. She described him as:

- About 18 years old.
- About 5ft 8in tall.
- Slim build.
- Fair and straight hair.
- Small face.
- Fair complexion.
- Ordinary type ears.
- Clean shaven.
- Well dressed and wearing a single breasted suit, shirt and tie.

The youth that she saw, allegedly the butcher, was later tried for Annie O'Donnell's murder but acquitted.

She said that she had never seen him before and that he didn't appear to see her at first. She said that he was standing at the west footway at the junction.

Clerkenwell Road

She said that the reason she was looking out of her window was because her son, who should have been home at 6pm, had not arrived.

She said that the youth had been standing at the junction and that after a couple of seconds he started to cross the road and that she noticed that he was touching his face with what appeared to be a cloth and walking to the opposite side and then back again and that he gave her the impression that he was nervous and she became suspicious of him.

She said that her husband had gone to the police station to see if anything had happened to her son and that after watching the youth opposite the flats she decided to go and find her husband to see what was happening and that in doing so she passed the youth in the middle of the road and that as she passed she looked straight at him. She noted that she later spoke to her husband and found that he had also seen the youth.

She noted that when she got to Hatton Garden that she found her husband at Slade & Woolf's and that it took her a couple of minutes to get there and she had a short conversation with him after which she noted that Banda's, the watch people's clock, said 8pm.

She said that when she came back the youth had gone.

The woman later attended an identification parade on 16 October 1962 at 1.45pm at Gray's Inn Police Station. She noted that although she had looked at him in the road, that she felt that she would not know the man for certain again. She said that there was only one man in the identification parade that she had to look at several times, who had in fact been the butcher, stating that he had fitted exactly the height, build and general appearance of the youth that she had seen, however, she didn't identify him as the person she had seen. although the fact that she had hesitated at him and none of the other men was noted in the police case.

Banda's clock

The police report noted that in fact, Banda's clock had three faces, with one of them facing Hatton Gardens, the one the woman saw, another facing Farringdon Road, which was also seen by the man that saw the unknown blonde woman in the shop, and the third, facing Clerkenwell Road, towards Gray's Inn Road.

However, it was noted that the clock faces were known to be unreliable, with each face showing a different time. When the secretary of Banda Limited, at 136 Clerkenwell Road was interviewed, she said that the clocks were unreliable and it was noted that although the clocks had been put right on the morning her statement was taken, that by the time she was interviewed, the faces showed:

1. Towards Farringdon Road: 3 minutes fast.
2. Towards Hatton Garden: 1 minute fast.
3. Towards Gray's Inn Road: 1 minute slow.

Man That Saw Unknown Blonde Woman In Shop

The man that saw the unknown blonde woman in the shop had also seen the clock on the day of the murder, and noted that it was wrong. He said that it had been the fifth time that he had visited Annie O'Donnell's shop and had done so on each occasion with a woman friend, and that each visit had been on a Friday and usually around 5.30pm and had lasted about half an hour or probably a little more.

He said that as you entered the shop that there was a counter that ran down the middle of the shop on the right with a small table adjoining on which goods were displayed. He said that there was a narrow gap between the table and the gas stove that was against the wall and that it was in that gap that Annie O'Donnell stood facing the table whenever he visited her. He noted that she would, of course, move from that position to get goods from cupboards or shelves, but that for conversation she always took up that position. He added that it was in that position that he was stood in when he entered the shop on 12 October 1962 and also when he left.

He said that he had followed his woman friend into the shop at about 5.30pm and that she walked along the counter looking at the display goods after having spoken to Annie O'Donnell. He said that he then put his package and raincoat down on a chair that stood on the left side and turned and faced the counter and that at that moment Annie O'Donnell left her position and walked behind the counter and joined his woman friend at the far end of the counter.

He said that as he faced the counter that his attention was drawn immediately to a clean sheet of what appeared to be plastic coated paper with unusual colouring, and that having studied photography for two and a half years he was immediately interested and pulled it towards him and looked at the picture. He said that it appeared to have been a printer's 'throw-out', noting that the colour was blue/green and that it appeared to have been a double print. He said that the sheet had been lying on top of a miscellaneous assortment of goods that were on display on the table and that there had been a crease in the paper but that apart from that it was perfectly clean.

He said that he was later shown a piece of paper at New Scotland Yard that was identical in every respect, down to the crease, with the exception that it then had marks, figures and had been treated in some way.

He said that on none of the previous occasions that he had visited Annie O'Donnell's shop that the piece of paper or similar paper had been on the little table or the counter and that he had not seen that sort of paper in the shop before at all. He said that there had been nothing on top of the paper at all and that that was its condition and position when he left the shop at 6.05pm.

He noted that he knew it was 6.05pm when he left because when they went outside into Clerkenwell Road his watch, which was accurate, showed seven and a half minutes past six. He further noted that two other clocks in the road showed different times, with Banda's clock showing 6.15pm, the face looking towards Farringdon Road, whilst the clock on the opposite side of the road showed between nine and ten minutes past six. He said that is woman friend had pointed out that it had been 6.15pm which was why he looked at his watch, which he knew was accurate.

Brother Of Woman From 9-10 Victoria Buildings

The brother of the woman who lived at 9-10 Victoria Buildings, a 19-year-old cabinet maker with no traced convictions, who lived at 38 Catherine House in Phillip Street, said that he visited his sister's address, 9-10 Victoria Gardens, at about 7.15pm on 12 October 1962. He said that upon finding that she was concerned about her son who had not returned home yet, that he went off to Hatton Garden to look for him and got as far as Slade & Woolf Limited where the son had been employed and found that it was in darkness.

He said that he then returned to 9-10 Victoria Buildings and a short time later went out again, upon which occasion he saw a man who he knew as Bobby Regan, the butcher, standing on the corner of Herbal Hill and

Clerkenwell Road outside the religious shop. He said that he was certain of his identification as he had known Bobby Regan for about seven years since they were schoolboys and had seen him from time to time over the years since. However, he noted that he was not friendly with the youth and didn't speak to him.

He said that he went on but still found no sign of his sister's son and so went back to 9-10 Victoria Buildings, noting that Bobby Regan was still outside the shop. He said that shortly after he came out again with his sister and that Bobby Regan was still outside the shop. He said that he then crossed Clerkenwell Road with his sister and then stood on the opposite side of Clerkenwell Road whilst his sister continued on to Hatton Garden.

He said that he then re-crossed Clerkenwell Road, at which time Bobby Regan was still there and went to his car in Herbal Hill and took a book from it and went back to 9-10 Victoria Buildings and told his aunt that he would then visit some other relatives to look for his sister's son. He said that he then drove to 32 Emberton Court in St John Street, visited another sister and then went home, but having failed to find the missing son, he went back to 9-10 Victoria Buildings, by which time the person he knew as Bobby Regan was gone.

He said that after visiting his sister's flat that he then walked back up Clerkenwell Road where he noticed a police officer put a piece of paper on a car windscreen, which it was stated fixed the time that that happened to be 8.30pm.

It was noted that the woman's brother initially gave times that he later agreed were incorrect, and stated two definite times, the first being 7.30pm when he had gone out, just after a television programme had commenced, and then later at 8.30pm, when he saw the police constable put the warning notice on the car, which was proved by the police constable that did it.

In an effort to establish the correct time when the brother saw Bobby Regan outside the shop, the police accompanied him on the car journey he said he took, it being noted that his estimate of 15 minutes for the journey was wrong, with it later being agreed that the journey took 25 minutes, which it was noted would have brought the last sighting of Bobby Regan back to 8.00pm, which was getting nearer to the time when his sister was in Hatton Garden.

The brother described the person he knew as Bobby Regan as:

- 19 years of age.
- 5ft 8in tall.
- Fresh complexion.
- Slim build.
- Thin face and nose.
- Wearing a light grey suit.

The police stated that they thought that the brother had been wrong about the suit, but noted that he had known the man as Bobby Regan for years and had seen him many times over the years. The brother told the police that Bobby Regan had attended the Hugh Myddleton School and had used to live in Clerkenwell Close, EC1 with his father and mother but that he believed he had since moved from that house but still lived in the neighbourhood. The brother said that the last time that he saw Bobby Regan before 12 October 1962 was about three weeks earlier in a barber's shop in Clerkenwell Close.

As such, the police report stated that it could be fairly said that the brother knew Bobby Regan extremely well and that there could be no possible doubt, irrespective of the clothing, of an accurate identification.

Enquiries To Trace Bobby Regan

The police then made immediate enquiries to trace Bobby Regan. It was noted that there had been a large family named Regan in the locality who were bookmakers and owned a number of betting shops, however, it was finally determined that Bobby Regan was not a member of that family. Other Regans were also seen and interviewed, but none answered the description of the man seen outside the shop.

Enquiries were also made at the barber's shop mentioned by the brother in Clerkenwell Close, but with no luck. The police also visited all addresses in Clerkenwell Close, but could not trace him and also stopped all young men and women in the area, but still to no avail.

In connection with this, on Sunday 14 October 1962, a detective constable and a police constable were in plain clothes in Farringdon Road near Clerkenwell Close when they saw the butcher. They stopped him and asked, 'Are you Bobby Regan?', but he replied 'No'. However, it was noted that his real name was not Bobby Regan, although it was similar. The butcher then joined three other men in a van and the driver of the van asked, 'What's the trouble governor?', and the detective constable said, 'We are police officers making enquiries into the murder of the old lady in Clerkenwell Road last Friday night. I wonder if any of you know a chap named Bobby Regan'. However, all three of the men said 'No', although the butcher said nothing. The four men then left on an outing to Brighton that they had arranged previously.

House to house enquiries were continued in Clerkenwell Close on Monday 15 October 1962 and at 10.15am two detectives called at 4 Clerkenwell Close and spoke to the butcher. They asked him:

We are making enquiries to trace a young man named Bobby Regan who is believed to have lived in this area. Do you know anyone of that name?

To which the butcher replied:

No. The only Regans I know here are the betting shop people. Is this about the murder?

The detectives said that it was about the murder and asked whether he could help, but he replied:

No. I've already had a pull by the law.

The man then went on to explain that he had gone on the outing and that he had not gone into work that day as he felt a bit rough. The police then left him after asking him to call them if he heard anything.

However, it was later found that the occupier of 4 Clerkenwell Close was a man whose son, the butcher, was also known as Bobby and that he had attended the Hugh Hyddleton School and that they had in fact lived next door to the barbers shop which itself was actually 4 Clerkenwell Close.

Later that day, at 5.15pm the police went back to the address and saw the butcher and told him that he matched the description of the Bobby Regan they were looking for. When they asked him where he had been the previous Friday night, he replied:

Herbal Hill

I got home from work about six o'clock, had some tea and a wash up and went out with my missus about half seven. We went to the Three Crowns and the Red Lion. I met a lot of my mates and we were drinking until closing time.

The police then asked him to come to the station to be interviewed, at which point the man's father intervened, asking, 'What's all this about?'. The police then told him that they were making enquiries about the murder in

Clerkenwell Road and that their superintendent would like a word with his son. However, the man's father said:

He isn't going to the police station. If your governor wants to see him tell him to come here.

The man's mother then came to the door and said:

He isn't leaving here with you.

The detectives then said, 'very well', and left.

In consequence of that, at 5.45pm, a detective inspector and a detective sergeant, went to 4 Clerkenwell Close and spoke to the man's father, behind whom the butcher was standing on the stairs. However, when they asked whether it was true that he would not allow his son to attend the police station he denied it, and replied:

No, that's wrong. What I said was he is not going to see anyone unless I'm with him.

He was then told that there would be no objection to that and he agreed to come along with his son.

The man then went upstairs and returned shortly after wearing a suede and wool jacket. The two detectives then left the house and went to their car whilst the man and his father went to a newsagent's shop nearby, with the father going in and his son waiting outside, after which they joined the detectives and were driven to Gray's Inn Road.

Butcher's Statement

The man was then interviewed and asked to account for his movements on Friday 12 October 1962, and in short, he denied having been in the immediate vicinity of the shop on the day of the murder.

He said:

I have been asked to explain my movements on Friday, 12th October, 1962.

About 2.20pm I went from home to the Red Lion public house at Rosoman Street and just looked in the saloon bar but saw no-one in there that I knew. I continued on to the Three Crowns public house, Rosebery Avenue, and looked in the bar. I asked the man behind the bar if any of my friends had been in there. I was looking for my friends because of an outing we had arranged for Sunday, 14th October. The man behind the bar said my friends had not been there.

From there I went to a friend's house in Percival Street, N1 and I stayed indoors with him until 4.20pm when we went out and got a bus to Chapel Street. There we went into Woolworth's to get a couple of combs, then after that we went into Littlewood's and there had a cup of tea.

We left there and walked through again to the corner of Rosoman Street and it must have been about 5.15pm when we arrived there. We waited on the corner for the Red Lion to open and while we were waiting a friend came along and joined us. Shortly after another friend came along and waited with us until the Red Lion opened and we all went in. Whilst we were in the public house another friend came in. I went in the public house with these men until 6.30pm or 6.45pm when I went home.

I had a wash and clean up then I went for a walk round with my wife. Whilst I was indoors my father and mother and also my wife were present the whole time. My wife and I occupy rooms on the ground and second floor at 4 Clerkenwell Close. My father and mother have the first floor rooms, so that when I went to clean up I had to go upstairs and looked in. My mother was watching television and my father was in the kitchen. Both of them saw me at that time.

I returned downstairs to my wife and at about 8.15pm I took her out for a walk. I went out of the house with her past the Horseshoe, round the other side of Northampton Buildings, through Hugh Myddleton School then through the Court which faces the Red Lion, past the Red Lion, up Rosoman Street and Finch's at the corner of Exmouth Street, crossed the road at the traffic lights and we both went into the Three Crowns public house where I was due to meet my friends regarding the outing to Brighton on Sunday.

Two friends were in there, then about 9pm to 9.15pm others came in. In all, apart from the two I mentioned there were eight of us together, along with the wives of those who were married. There were four unmarried men. We remained there until closing time, 11pm, then the wife and I went home.

I am a Roman Catholic by religion but I do not attend St Peter's Church. I know the shop at Clerkenwell Road selling religious statues. The only time I was in there was about three weeks before I got married which was on 26th May 1962. I went there to get a rosary for my wife.

At no time on Friday was I in Clerkenwell Road standing in the vicinity of the religious shop. By vicinity I mean standing outside the shop. I maintain I was not standing outside that shop on Friday, 12th October 1962.

When I bought the rosary I was served by an old lady who was the only person there. It cost me about fifteen shillings. I gave her a £1 note. I cannot be sure but I remember she took the change from an apron or overall type of garment. I did not know her and this was the only time I saw her.

The police summarised his explanation by stating that there was no doubt that until 6.30pm to 6.45pm the man had been with friends in public houses. They continued by noting that he claimed he then went directly home where he remained until 8.15pm, which his parents and wife all supported, after which he said he took his wife for a walk round the streets until they arrived at the Three Crowns public house in Tysoe Street, Rosebery Avenue, which in effect constituted the extent of his alibi.

The police noted that they checked the times to cover the routes described by the man, finding that even walking at a very slow pace, the route taken by the man and his wife only took ten minutes and five seconds.

They also timed the journey walking at a normal pace from 32 Victoria Buildings to his home address, 4 Clerkenwell Close, and found that the longest time was two minutes fifty seconds, during which journey they crossed Vine Street Bridge, under which the documents in the name of Annie O'Donnell were found on the railway line.

Further Questioning

The police report highlighted vital parts of the interview with the butcher, first in which a detective said:

I want to be perfectly fair with you. That is why your father is here looking after your interests. I want you to be very careful about what I am going to ask you. You have given an account of your movements from two o'clock till eleven o'clock on Friday, 12th October, yet I have reason to believe that you were outside the shop in Clerkenwell Road where the old lady was murdered.

To which the butcher replied:

No, I was not there.

The detective then said to him:

Now let's get this quite clear. Your movements are supported by independent witnesses up to 6.45pm and again from roughly 9pm yet during the vital times we are mainly concerned with your only witnesses are your parents up to a point and your wife, with whom you say you were walking round the streets. Do you still maintain you were not outside the shop at any time that day?

To which the butcher replied:

I wasn't there.

The interview continued:

Detective: So that we do not have any misunderstanding at all, do you know the shop we are talking about?

Butcher: Yes.

Detective: Have you ever been in the shop?

Butcher: No.

Butcher (almost immediately after): Wait a minute, I have. I went in to buy a rosary for my wife.

Detective: When was this?

Butcher: Five or six months ago. I got married in May. It was about three weeks before that. I took it straight into the church next door and the priest blessed it.

Detective: Who served you?

Butcher: The old lady.

Detective: How much did you pay for it?

Butcher: About fifteen bob.

Detective: How did you pay for it?

Butcher: What do you mean?

Detective: Did you give a note or the right money?

Butcher: Oh, a pound note.

Detective: Where did she put it and get the change from?

Butcher: I think it was a sort of apron.

Detective: Now finally, have you ever been in the shop on any other occasion either before you bought the rosary or since?

Butcher: No, never.

The butcher then made his statement.

It was noted however, that apart from the period for which the man could not account by independent witnesses, there was nothing to connect him with the murder, so much so that the police said they had doubts as to the wisdom of keeping him at the station overnight pending the holding of an identification parade. However, after questioning the brother of the woman who lived at 9-10 Victoria Dwellings, who said he had seen the person he knew as Bobby Regan, they decided to keep the man overnight in order that the identification parade could be held, it being noted that efforts had been made to hold one that night, but without success.

The police added that it was also necessary to check his story and statements were taken from his parents and wife.

The Butcher's father

The butcher's father, who had nine convictions for crime including two for assault occasioning actual bodily harm, said that he was employed as a painter and got home from work on the evening of 12 October 1962 at about 6.15pm and had his tea, after which, at about 6.40pm, his son looked into his room. He said that he then heard him go upstairs and then later come down to the ground floor where he heard him talking to his wife and then sometime later heard him call out, 'See you later', before going out, noting that he assumed that his wife had accompanied him, because he didn't see her again later.

The Butcher's Mother

The man's mother said that her son stayed in all day until 7.30pm apart from an hour in the afternoon when he took his younger brother out.

She said that he went out at 7.30pm for a walk and a drink and didn't return until 12.30am on 13 October 1962. She said that when he went out he had been wearing his suede jacket, although other witnesses were traced to say that he had been wearing his blue suit.

The Butcher's Wife

The man's wife said that her husband went out at about 2.45pm and returned about 6.45pm after which they had tea together and stayed in until about 8pm when they went out for a walk together. However, it was noted that when she was asked what streets they had walked through, she couldn't say, and became very distressed when pressed on the point.

She continued to state that they went to the Three Crowns public house and then to a restaurant in Edgeware Road with another man, after which they returned home, had some tea and went to bed at 2am.

She said, in conflict with other witnesses, that when her husband first went out, her husband had been wearing his suede jacket and jeans, but changed into his blue suit to go out later.

She added that her husband gave her a rosary about a week before their marriage on 26 May 1962, which she produced. At first she didn't want to part with it, but later that same day agreed to hand it over to a detective.

She said that her husband had not given her any money for that week, the week of the murder, and that she herself worked and earned about £8 a week.

It was noted that at the time of the interview, the man's wife had had no money. She said that for the week of the murder she only had £3 and had spent that on errands.

It was also noted that at the time she had been heavily pregnant, with the child being expected in mid-November 1962.

Other Men Claimed To Have Been On Night Out With Suspect

The police report noted that the butcher mentioned a number of men that had been in his company on the day of the murder, however, they were only able to immediately trace one of them. He was a 26-year-old man who supported the man's story from approximately 5.15pm until 6.45pm and then again from 9pm till 1am. He initially said that he had left home to go to the Three Crowns at about 8.30pm and had been there for about half-an-hour when the man came in with his wife and that they all stayed until closing time.

He said then that he later left the Three Crowns public house with the butcher and his wife and went to a club in Edgeware Road where they had a bottle of gin and sandwiches, noting that they travelled there and back by taxi cab. He said that apart from giving the man £2 for his share and paying for some extra bottles of tonic water, the man paid all other expenses.

However, the 26-year-old man then became very difficult and most elusive. On Friday 19 October 1962 the police spoke to him on the phone and made an appointment to meet him at Bow Street police station at 12 noon that day, but a few moments later the man telephoned again to say that he had spoken to his solicitor who had told him not to keep the appointment.

The police then called the solicitor, who denied having told the 26-year-old man not to keep the appointment. However, the police managed to see the 26-year-old man the following day, at which point he claimed that the man tried and his wife had already been in the Three Crowns public house when he arrived on the evening of Friday 12 October 1962, after having himself visited two other public houses first.

He said that when he entered the Three Crowns that he saw the man's wife sitting in the bar, but didn't see her husband until sometime later when he appeared in the company.

He also stated that the man had been wearing his blue suit on both the occasions that they were in each other's company on the day.

However, the police report stated that it was reasonable to conclude that the 26-year-old man would support the butcher regardless of where the truth of the matter might lie, or who called him as a witness, and that it was their opinion that he would crumble under cross-examination and that whatever his testimony amounted to, it would be of doubtful value to whoever called him.

Delayed Identity Parade

Due to court commitments of the solicitor for the butcher, it was not possible to hold the identification parade at 10am and it was delayed until 1pm.

When the butcher was in the detention room a detective cautioned him and told him that they wanted to clear up a few points following the interview with the 26-year-old man, noting that he had told them that he had gone home after leaving the Three Crowns public house, to which the man replied:

No, we didn't. That's right. We went to a club in the Edgeware Road for a drink and a sandwich.

He then added that he had been accompanied by his wife and the 26-year-old man.

He agreed that they had bought a bottle of gin, but stressed that it had been between them and that they didn't finish it and instead took the remainder home. He also stated that they took a cab to and from Edgeware Road and that he had paid for the drinks, sandwiches and cab fare, estimating that the evenings expenditure was 'about seven or eight quid'.

When it was pointed out to him that he had been away from work and asked whether he had drawn any wages, he replied, 'No'. When he was then asked where he had got the money, he replied, 'I had it put by'.

He was then asked about the rosary he had bought his wife and asked whether she had been a Roman Catholic, and he replied, no, but that her parents were and that she had wanted to carry a rosary at her wedding.

In the interim, arrangements were made for suitable persons to be found to stand on the parade. It was noted that the brother that had seen the man he knew as Bobby Regan, had said he had been wearing a grey suit and officers were instructed to get men dressed in grey suits. However, the ones they obtained were either dressed in dark grey or blue and faintly striped suits. Further, the man's suit, nearest to light grey, which was in fact a mixture of colours, green and light brown check, had been given to him to wear, with his other blue suit being at the laboratory.

Before the man was introduced to the parade the detective and the solicitor went to see the men that were to form the parade as they had anticipated objections from the solicitor and had more men standing by, and in fact the solicitor did object, noting that the man had been wearing a light suit whilst all the other men were wearing dark clothing. The detective said that he agreed immediately and the man's parents brought a change of clothing, a dark brown woollen cardigan coat and dark brown trousers, which the man's solicitor was said to have been well satisfied with. However, when the detective saw what the man was dressed in he immediately objected and the parade was again delayed until the man's blue suit could be brought from the laboratory.

Looking along Clerkenwell Road

When it arrived, the parade commenced at 1.45pm and the butcher was put in amongst the other men who were all of a similar age, height and general appearance.

When the woman that lived at 9-10 Victoria Dwellings was introduced, she walked quickly down the line of men, hesitated near the butcher, but then turned her back and walked back to the inspector and said, 'No'.

When she was questioned after the parade, she said that the butcher had looked like the man she had seen, so much so that she had to look again, and that all the other men in the parade stated that she only hesitated in front of the suspect.

It was further noted that there was no doubt that the woman had in fact attended the parade with reluctance, and had since adopted an attitude of wishing she had not become involved in the case, with it further being noted that she had attempted to alter her appearance by borrowing clothing to wear on the parade.

However, when her brother was brought into the parade, he stood at an angle at the end of the parade and without hesitation said:

Third one up from the end.

Which was the position occupied by the suspect. However, that didn't satisfy the inspector who asked him to point to him, and so the brother pointed to and touched the suspect on the chest, saying that he had been the man he had seen outside the shop on the day in question.

Following The Identification of Bobby Regan

Following the identification of the suspect as Bobby Regan, the man the brother saw outside the shop, the police said that they were still faced with an impasse as there was still no evidence to connect him with the murder. He was then detained whilst further enquiries were made at his address, however, nothing of any evidential value was found there.

Up until that time the other associates of the butcher had not been traced and the police were having difficulty finding them, but that the very next evening they all attended the office of the butcher's solicitor and made their statements collectively, and the police submitted that there was little doubt that the minds of each of the men had been conditioned as to the times that they mentioned.

They were:

1. 26-year-old man. Had already given evidence about meeting the butcher in the Three Crowns and later going to the club with him and his wife.
2. Marine store dealer, 151 Whitfield Street. Said he was in the Red Lion with the butcher until 6.45pm and later saw him between 8.30pm and 9.00pm at the Three Crowns.
3. Asphalt constructor, 137 Buckingham Street, Islington. Said he saw the butcher in the Three Crowns at about 9pm. Added that he collected £1 from him for the outing on Sunday.
4. Painter, 12 Chanston House, Halton Road, N1. Said he went to the Three Crowns at about 8.45pm and that the butcher and his wife were already there. Added that he went to Brighton with the butcher on Sunday 14 October 1962 with others.
5. Plumber's mate, 107 Grimthorpe House, Ogden Street, EC1. Said he was with the butcher from 5.45pm to 6.45pm in the Red Lion and later arrived at the Three Crowns about 8.45pm to find the butcher and his wife already there.
6. Lift engineer's mate, 18 Tompion House, Percival Street, EC1. Said he had been with the butcher from about 3.00pm to 6.30pm and later arrived at the Three

Crowns about 8.45pm to 9.00pm to find the butcher and his wife already there. He said that he stayed at the Three Crowns until closing time and that they all had a whip round of ten shillings to a pound to go to a party.

7. Meat porter, 2 Javens Chambers, 112 Clerkenwell Road. Said he had been with the butcher in the Red Lion at 6.40pm and that the butcher left almost immediately afterwards. He said that he then later went to the Three Crowns at about 8.45pm to 8.50pm to find the butcher and his wife already there.

The licensee of the Three Crowns said that he could only say that the butcher had been in his house with his wife that night but could not state when he arrived or when he first saw him.

The licensee's wife said that when she came downstairs at 9pm, that the butcher and his wife were in the bar.

Searches on the butcher's associates were made at the Criminal Record Office, but there was no trace of any of them there.

It was noted that three other men that had been with the group were not traced by the police although it was believed that they had been spoken to by the butcher's solicitor.

Fingerprint Evidence

After the identification parade, during the afternoon, information was received from the fingerprint department at New Scotland Yard that fingerprints had been found on the sheet of glazed paper, which was in fact a printer's 'throw out', that was found on the table at the shop and which were identical to that of the butcher.

It was noted that the sheet was shown in 'photograph 4' in the evidence album, on the 'table' counter extension in the left background with its front corner folded up. The sheet of paper was printed on partially with a two-colour illustration advertising 'Bri-Nylon'.

Immediate enquiries were made to establish the origin of the paper, and how it arrived at Annie O'Donnell's shop, and it was later traced to Linear Litho Ltd, a lithographic plate maker in Exmouth House, Pine Street, EC1. The manager there said that until 7 May 1962, they had occupied premises at 151 Farringdon Road, which was no great distance from Victoria Dwellings and he identified the paper as having been processed by his company, referring to it as 'printer's waste'. He said that the order for that job had been received by his company on 13 March 1961 and the order completed by 27 March 1961.

He said that during the proofing of the plates used for the printing, that forty or fifty sheets of paper were used from which the best were selected and trimmed and sent to the customer with the plates, with the remainder of the paper left at the street entrance in Farringdon Road for collection by the refuse collectors.

As such, it was stated that it was obvious that the paper could have been collected by some person, or even Annie O'Donnell, some eighteen months before the murder. It was further noted that the main suspect had claimed to have had legitimate access to the customer side of Annie O'Donnell's shop in early May 1962.

It was noted that against that, 21 rolls of similar waste paper and one package enclosed in cardboard covers was found behind the shop counter and that none of that paper was found on the customers side of the counter apart from a few sheets scattered on the floor, apparently at the time of the murder.

The police also stated that the paper must have been resting on a hard surface for the impressions to have been left, such as it was in photograph 4 of the evidence album.

It was then recalled that the man that had been in the shop and seen the paper on the table shortly before the murder said that he had taken an interest in it because of his interest in colour photography and that he had pulled it towards him and looked at it and found that it was clean and apparently new, with a crease in it. He further noted that he had been to the shop four times before and never noticed the paper on those earlier occasions.

A woman that had been visiting the shop at least twice a month for the previous five years said that she had never before seen similar paper there. She said that when she called on 12 October 1962, she recalled seeing the paper on top of articles on the table, and that she had placed her shopping bag on top of it. She said that it had appeared to be new and unmarked, apart from the crease.

She later identified the paper at New Scotland Yard, but noted that it had at that time had some markings on it, which appeared to have been made by Annie O'Donnell in calculating a price. The markings were:

4 - 4 -
4 - 4 -
13 -
Cru & Cha 1 - 10 -
----
10 - 11 -
£10 - 11 -

It was noted that no definite explanation had been placed on the figures, but that it seemed that the 'Cri & Cha' was an abbreviation for crucifix and chain.

It was noted that the figures and letters did not touch the finger prints found on the paper, although certain of the marks were underneath blood from Annie O'Donnell, although experiments as to the certainty of that factor were still being made.

Butcher Charged

The butcher was charged with murder on 17 October 1962 at 10.53am in the presence of his solicitor. When he was cautioned he made no reply. When he was charged shortly after at 11.15am, he said:

I am not guilty of this matter. I have got nothing to do with the matter in any way.

More Fingerprints Found

Following being charged, the police found further fingerprints on a copy of the Catholic Herald, dated 5 October 1962, that was also on the table and to be seen in photograph four, which were found through the use of Ninhydrin, a chemical process for the development of latent prints on paper. It was then noted that the significance of the find was such that unless the man changed his story, his defence of legitimate access to the shop was now not open to him.

It was noted that the Catholic Herald had been a weekly newspaper printed in High Wycombe and published from 67 Fleet Street where the London end of the distribution was dealt with, the paper being received from the printers on Thursday mornings, just after midnight. It was further noted that there had been a standing order for 26 copies to be delivered every week to the Italian Church (St Peter's), in Clerkenwell Road.

Enquiries were made of all newsagents in the area, but no trace could be made of Annie O'Donnell having had an order for the newspaper and it was thought more probable that Annie O'Donnell had obtained her copy from the church itself, where the papers were left stacked and customers helped themselves and left their money in a coin slot near the newspapers. However, no witnesses were found who could say they saw Annie O'Donnell buying the newspaper.

The delivery of the newspapers to the church was found to have been made on 4 October 1962 at about 9am.

Motive

It was assumed that robbery had been the motive for the murder, as the cupboards and drawers had been ransacked. It was thought that the items found on the railway line had been thrown away by the robber and noted that no money was found on the premises other than that found in the tins and in Annie O'Donnell's money belt.

It was noted that there must have been a number of customers in the shop in 12 October 1962, but that only two had been traced.

One customer, a man from 12 Worcester Court in Deansgate, said that he purchased two rosaries for 14/- and paid by cheque drawn on the Midland Bank Ltd, but the cheque was not paid in and was found to be missing following the murder.

The other customers were the man and woman that had seen the piece of paper on the table and seen the unknown blonde woman in the shop when they left. They noted that they paid Annie O'Donnell £1 against an order that she was holding for them and that Annie O'Donnell had made an entry for it in her invoice book, dated 12 October 1962. However, although the invoice book was found, there was no trace of the £1 that had been handed to Annie O'Donnell. The woman noted that Annie O'Donnell had put the £1 into a bag with a drawstring, similar to a bank bag, but no trace of the bag was found either.

The woman also noted that when she had been in the shop that she had noticed two large brass candlesticks, like those used in churches, standing on the counter towards the far side, but no trace of them was ever made.

The last two known customers said that when they left that a blonde woman had come into the shop. They described her as:

- Aged 30 - 35.
- 5ft 3in tall.
- Plump build.
- Small nose.
- Short blonde hair.
- Dressed in either a dark green or blue coat of raglan style.

The police said that they were anxious to trace the woman to establish the reason for her visit and any possible explanation for the figures and writing on the sheet of paper, as well as any other customers that had been in the shop that day. To that end the police made an appeal through the national press and the BBC radio, but with no response. However, it was noted that the appeal was made during the early stages of the Cuban crisis and was not considered front page news.

A Possible Accomplice

It was noted that in the early stages of the investigation that the police reported that there were two suspects, after they spoke to a garage hand employed at Modern Motors Limited in Clerkenwell Road, on the opposite side of the road to the junction of Herbal Hill who had said that he had seen some girls across the road between 8pm and 8.30pm and then noticed two men standing talking near to the first entrance to Victoria Dwellings, that being the common entrance leading to the shop.

The garage hand had not been able to see their features, but described them as being 28/30, 5ft 8in, medium build and that one of them had been wearing a light coloured raincoat.

The police constable that was seen by the brother to place a warning notice on a car said that he had been in the vicinity at the time dealing with a burglar alarm ringing in Hatton Garden near the junction of Clerkenwell Road. It was recalled that he had placed the warning notice on the car at 8.30pm. He stated that at about 8.35pm he saw two men standing at the corner of Herbal Hill and Clerkenwell Road, one of whom he took to be the woman's brother, who he said had been wearing a red 'V' neck pullover, and it was determined that the woman's brother had in fact been wearing a red 'V' neck jumper that night. As such, it was considered that that had been when the brother had returned from his search for the son and had already stated in his evidence that the man he identified as Bobby Regan had gone.

It was also noted that a woman who lived at 62 Victoria Dwellings had seen a man, about 40-years-old at about 7.50pm walking away from the shop along with two other men that she had seen walking near to the church, one of whom she described as being very tall and the other short and Italian looking and wearing a dark suit and black winkle-picker shoes, whom the police said no significance was attached to, but noted that the woman had obviously spoken to the press who had described the men seen by her in the papers. The police described all the other men reported in the newspapers as red-herrings.

Butcher's Antecedent History

The police report noted that the butcher had been employed as a butcher at a branch of CF Freeman Ltd, 10 Berwick Street. He was described as a good workman but a bad timekeeper. He had been employed since 28 August 1962 and the amounts he had been paid were detailed as:

- 31 August: £4.0.9d net.
- 7 September: £12.5.8d net.
- 14 September: £9.2.2d net.
- 21 September: £12.12.1d net.
- 28 September: £6.16.0d net.
- 5 October: £12.0.6d net.

He was also noted as having been due to draw wages of £5.5.4d, which he had not collected since he went sick and noted that the figures were not in keeping with his claim, when questioned, about money he had spent, and him having 'had some put away'.

Laboratory Evidence

It was noted that both Annie O'Donnell and the man tried were blood group A, and that as such, a small spot of blood found on the man's right trouser pocket of his suit was of no value either for the prosecution or the defence.

Conclusion Of Police Report

The conclusion of the police report stated that there was no doubt that the man identified as Bobby Regan was responsible for the murder. However, he was cleared after two trials with the prosecution offering no evidence at a third trial. The conclusion of the police report read:

This was a particularly vicious and brutal murder, with robbery quite clearly the motive. It was done with calm deliberation and not in a panic during the course of what was intended to be merely robbery.

An old lady, harmless and quite defenceless who had spent her life in the service of the church, was struck down, savagely battered, murdered and robbed amidst the emblems of her religion whilst preparing to attend her church for a special service known as the 'Stations of the Cross'.

There is no doubt that the butcher was the perpetrator of this vile crime for the sake of a few pounds he must have taken from the dying body of this old lady. Following this he ransacked the cupboard and drawers in the shop, and with the proceeds went to a public house where he joined or was joined by his wife and companions and remained there drinking until the place closed. During this time he made final arrangements with friends for an outing to Brighton the following Sunday, and then with his pregnant wife and a friend went to a club in Edgeware Road, where they purchased a bottle of gin.

What was this 18-year-old married man celebrating? He had drawn no wages for that week, yet on his own admission had spent between seven or eight pounds on the day of the murder. In addition he went on the outing the following Sunday, which quite obviously cost a few pounds. It may be of interest to note that when he was searched at this police station on Monday, 15th October, 1962, he possessed only ten shillings, and this he gave to his father to buy cigarettes.

There is little doubt that the fatal blows were delivered between 7.50pm and 8.00pm. The butcher has positively been identified as being outside the shop at the vital times, this in spite of repeated denials to me in the presence of his father that he was there at any time that day. The story that he was at home will no doubt be supported by his family.

How he will account for his finger and palm prints being in the shop, when this evidence is revealed, is not known, but I have no doubt that with the assistance of his well-known solicitor, some original or ingenious explanation must be anticipated.

It is our belief that the attack was made whilst the deafening bells of St Peter's Church were being tolled, calling the worshippers to church for the 8pm Benediction. This would account for her two neighbours, who were but a few feet away separated only by two flimsy wooden doors and the passageway, hearing nothing.

According to the pathologist, the first blow resulted in the injury shown in Page 4 of Album B. This would have caused her to put her hands to her head, and as she fell was probably struck further blows which caused the 'protective' injuries to the backs of the hands as shown in

Pages 6 and 7 of Album B. Having fallen to the floor, she was then subjected to a barrage of brutal and savage blows to either side and back of the head as shown on Pages 2, 3 and 5 of Album B.

The injuries inflicted were far more savage than were necessary to rob this old lady and indicate a premeditated murder by a cold and calculating person, the purpose probably being to prevent any question of identification at a later date, particularly in this case where it is possible that the butcher was known by Miss O'Donnell by sight.

Although this is clearly a murder done in the furtherance of theft, there is no direct evidence to show what was stolen. It is known that Mis O'Donnell had received a £1 note at about 6.05pm and a cheque for 14/- earlier that day. It is also quite reasonable to assume she had other customers , and in any event, must have carried some petty cash on her. Two witnesses described the drawstring type of bag she had. None of this property was in the shop or has been found. In addition personal documents bearing her name and address were found on the railway line 120 yards from her shop, and about midway on the direct route to the butcher's home, which is 150 yards further on.

When the butcher was arraigned at the Central Criminal Court on 6 February 1963, he admitted to having later been to her shop, but still denied any involvement in her murder, saying that he had been there two or three days prior to the murder as a potential customer.

Evidence for the prosecution consisted mainly of the following points:

1. He was identified by a man who knew him personally as being outside the shop at the material time.
2. His finger and palm impressions were found inside the shop.
3. Proof that these impressions had been made within the previous week.
4. Denials by him that he was outside the shop on the day in question, and had not been in those premises for six months.
5. Subsequent admission to police that he was at the scene of the crime but had not killed Miss O'Donnell.

The butcher denied having been involved with her murder and denied making any statement of admission to the police.

It was noted that when the butcher gave his evidence at the trial as to having been in the shop two or three days earlier, that it was the first that the prosecution had heard of the alleged and most opportune visit to the shop. He explained his reason for not revealing the visit to the police earlier as being due to the fact that in 1961 he had been convicted of stealing a ladder, and that that conviction was due to the police telling lies about him and that if he told the police about his more recent visit to the shop on 9 or 10 October 1962, that they would have:

re-arranged this visit to fit in with the murder on Friday 12th.

It was further noted that apart from his wife and parents, including his father who had many previous convictions which were not made known to the court, the butcher offered no other evidence.

The jury retired for five hours, but were unable to reach a verdict and were discharged.

The butcher was again arraigned at the Central Criminal Court on 27 February 1962, but the evidence for the Crown was fundamentally the same as the previous trial.

At the conclusion of the trial, the judge told the jury that they had four points to consider:

1. Whether or not the butcher had been at the scene, noting that if they found he wasn't that that meant an acquittal.
2. Point two was not detailed.
3. Point three was not detailed.
4. Point four was not detailed. It was noted that it was on the remaining three points on which it would depend whether the verdict would be one of, guilty of capital murder, ordinary murder or manslaughter.

However, after a retirement of some five and a half hours, the jury returned and said that they could not reach an agreement on the first point.

The butcher was arraigned again on 8 March 1963 at the Central Criminal Court for the third time, but the Crown offered no evidence and the butcher was acquitted with a formal not guilty verdict.

A later police report stated that it was quite impossible to suggest any logical reason why the two juries failed to reach a verdict after two trials lasting five days each.

The report stated that there was an abundance of evidence on which any unbiased jury could have safely convicted the butcher of either capital or non-capital murder, concluding that the point that that posed was whether they had had an unbiased jury, adding that there were grounds for believing that that was not to be so, for the following reasons:

The police report continued:

On 27th February, 1963, prior to the commencement of the second trial, I received information from a most reliable source, as a result of which I made application to the Director of Public Prosecutions' representative at the Central Criminal Court for the names etc of the jurymen. After some enquiry he told me this had been refused because he said there had already been some trouble with a similar request.

At the conclusion of this trial on 6th March, 1963, as the Court was beginning to clear, I received the following information. Thirty-three jurors had been empanelled from which the jury for the Mitcham murder were to be selected and as the result of searches at the Criminal Record Office it was discovered that between eight and twelve of them had criminal records. The Superintendent quite naturally objected to these men and the jury was formed from the remainder.

A second jury was formed for a case of rape in another court before a judge, and as this jury came to be sworn, those with convictions were objected to by Counsel for the prosecution. Eight jurors in all were objected to and this was allowed after some caustic comments. My informant told me that all (or some of these eight) formed part of my jury.

Upon receiving this information, I immediately went to the Clerk of No 2 Court and asked for the names of my jurors. He reminded me the case was over and asked why I wanted them. I related what I had been told and he said, 'There has been some trouble over juries. I cannot give you the names. You must apply to the Director.' I told him I had already been refused by the Director of

Public Prosecutions and he said 'I do not wish to discuss it with you'.

Looking along up Herbal Hill

I later pressed the Director of Public Prosecutions' representative for confirmation and he agreed that the story related above was basically true, excepting he assured me that when the eight had been rejected they did not serve on any other jury. I told this gentleman I was bound to accept his explanation, but to completely remove any misunderstanding, I still wanted the names of the jurors who served in our Court. Again I was refused. Thus the matter lies. Did we have a jury of unbiased men or did the jury include eight or less men with criminal convictions who had been rejected from service in a case of rape, yet accepted for service for a case of capital murder. The evasions and secrecy which is being drawn around their identities leaves me as personally in a little doubt that the story told by the informant is true.

There is no doubt that the butcher was the person who brutally murdered Miss O'Donnell for the few pounds she must have had in the shop.

To commit such a callous crime on a defenceless old woman, then to join his friends in a convivial evening on the proceeds, coupled with his apparent indifference throughout the subsequent police investigation and proceedings, stamps this man, despite his years, as a ruthless thug.

Perhaps the answer to the butcher's composure lies in his own words, for during the retirement of the second jury he was asked by one of the prison officers, 'How do you manage to remain so calm?'. His reply was, 'You must remember Guv, I am in the butchery trade'.

The response to the police report was:

I am not really in a position to comment on some of the matters raised in this report, except perhaps to say that I can see the ethical point followed in not supplying the names of jurymen to police after the trial.

What does strike me, and this could be the answer to the detective superintendent's criticism, is that it may well be that there are insufficient numbers of potential jurymen available at the Central Criminal Courts, for empanelling on juries, particularly on occasions such as this when there are three very important cases to be tried.

I appreciate that the Detective Superintendent should feel aggrieved at the decision in this case after all the hard work put into the investigation, but I cannot help feeling that we would be treading on very dangerous ground if we were to try and pursue this matter further, assuming that it were possible (and quite frankly I do not see how it is, as an approach has already been made to the Clerk of the Court and to the DPP representative without any result).

All in all, then, my view is that we should let sleeping dogs lie. No doubt there is a lesson to be learned from this as regards the composition of juries, although I know it is something which has bedevilled police prosecutions since time immemorial, and I cannot see that there is any ready answer to it.

After the trials, on Tuesday 23 April 1963, the police were called to 4 Clerkenwell Close by the butchers mother who she alleged had a few moment earlier severely cut his arm. A police constable at attended said:

I went to the second floor rear bedroom of the premises, where I saw the injured person lying on his back, behind the door, wearing only a pair of under pants. He was bleeding from a cut about three inches long, on his left forearm at the elbow joint which appeared to have been self-inflicted. He appeared to be unconscious.

The room appeared to be in order except for the bed which was unmade, some of the bedclothes being bloodstained. I told his mother to ring for an ambulance, and rendered first-aid until it arrived at 1.15am.

I accompanied the injured person in the ambulance to the Royal Free Hospital, Gray's Inn Road, WC1 during which time he appeared to remain unconscious. On arrival at the hospital he was examined and treated by a doctor and then detained.

On regaining consciousness at the hospital he became violent and had to be restrained. He said to me, 'What are you doing here?'. I said, 'How did you cut your arm?'. He said, 'You are wasting your time, I'm telling you nothing'. He appeared very belligerent and refused to make any further statement.

His mother said, 'We heard him fall off the bed and rushed upstairs and found him'. His wife said, 'He was annoyed with me. We had a quarrel. He had been upstairs for about five minutes and I came up and found him like this'.

His mother also informed me that her husband had been receiving treatment from his own doctor for a nervous condition. Whilst on the premises of 4 Clerkenwell Close, EC1, I made a search for the instrument used to inflict the wound without success, and members of the family said they did not know what it had been done with.

However, the doctor noted that his wound was not deep and didn't require stitching. Whilst it was first considered to have been a suicide attempt, on 13 May 1963 it was reported that it was not a serious attempt at suicide and rather just another demonstration of his extreme violence, and apart from an entry in the Occurrence Book, no further police action was deemed necessary or contemplated.

However, it was noted that it was only a short time after the incident that he was heard of again, on 3 May 1963 when he was arrested and charged at Rochester Row police station in the name of Morris Spillane, with assault with intent to rob a young woman at the passport office at Clive House, Petty France, SW1. For that he appeared at Bow Street magistrates court on 4 May 1963 until 13 May 1963 at which time he was committed to the Central Criminal Court commencing 21 May 1963 where he was finally convicted on 27 June 1963 and sentenced to 12 months imprisonment.

A detective at Rochester Row police station commented on the sentence in a report, stating:

It is gratifying that he was convicted on this occasion but it may be doubted whether a person of such violent propensities will learn much from a sentence of only 12 months imprisonment.

James Albert Kenyon

Age: 38

Sex: male

Date: 12 Oct 1962

Place: Wigan, Lancashire

James Albert Kenyon was killed in a street fight.

A man was tried for his murder but acquitted.

James Kenyon had been a paint sprayer and had lived at 38 Woodhouse Lane in Wigan.

He had been out to a dance hall and got involved in a scuffle, resulting in his death.

The man tried had been his friend and had been out with him on the night and said that when the scuffle started that he tried to restrain James Kenyon, however, he said that James Kenyon had resented that and used obscene language. Shortly after James Kenyon was seen chasing his friend up the road, the friend having decided to leave with his wife.

They were next seen behind a bus shelter were James Kenyon struck his friend twice, after which his friend hit him twice back, causing him to fall and hit his head on the pavement, fracturing his skull.

Joseph McEwan

Age: 23

Sex: male

Date: 10 Oct 1962

Place: Whitehall, Hampshire

Joseph McEwan died in a street fight in Whitehall near Bordon in Hampshire, on the night of 10 October 1962.

Three men were tried for his murder but it was impossible to say who was more blame worthy than who. However, they pleaded guilty to causing an affray. They were tried at the Hampshire Assizes on 11 December 1962.

Eight other men had also been charged with causing an affray in a public highway.

The fight was between soldiers and civilians, with a total of twenty people being involved. The court heard that after a dance by the Prince of Wales public house in Whitehall on 10 October 1962 that a number of local youths walked through a group of soldiers standing on the pavement outside, which it was said seemed to have led to the fight.

The event had been a 'Twist' session at the dance hall next to the Prince of Wales public house. It was heard that just after the dance ended at 11pm on the Wednesday night that Joseph McEwan said to the landlord, 'I enjoyed the dance. When is the next one?', but that a few minutes later the fight started.

Joseph McEwan had been a Private in the REME and had been from Shirsa Street in Glasgow.

The three men tried had been labourers, aged 18, 20 and 20.

Dennis Hurley

Age: 46

Sex: male

Date: 6 Oct 1962

Place: Marshgate Lane, Stratford, London

Dennis Hurley was knocked down during a scuffle in Stratford, London on 1 October 1962 and died in hospital five days later.

A 42-year-old man was tried for his manslaughter at the Old Bailey but acquitted.

It was heard that Dennis Hurley had had an abnormally thin skull. The 42-year-old man was said to have struck Dennis Hurley during an argument, causing him to fall down.

The 42-year-old man had been the chairman of the Stratford, branch of the Transport and General Workers Union.

Dennis Hurley had been Irish and had been a tanker driver and had lived in a flat in Junction Road, Romford with his wife, a 41-year-old office worker. They had had no children. They were described as a devoted couple.

It was heard that there had been a meeting of the Transport and General Workers Union members at Pickford's transport depot in Marshgate Lane, Stratford, which had been called because some drivers had been complaining about new time schedules for a long-distance run from a depot at Stanford-le-Hope, Essex. It was heard that some men started jeering when they objected to the way that a union official wanted to handle the dispute and that there was then a scuffle and Dennis Hurley fell to the ground, hitting his head and fracturing his skull.

He died in hospital on 6 October 1962. He arrived at Queen Mary Hospital unconscious and remained in a coma until he died.

Detectives and his wife had waited at his bedside since the Monday in case he regained consciousness.

Augustine P Dooley

Age: 45

Sex: male

Date: 9 Sep 1962

Place: Summer Road, Edgbaston

Augustine Dooley died from head injuries.

He had lived in Broad Lane, Coventry.

He died in the Birmingham General Hospital on 9 September 1962, a month after he injured his head.

He had attended a family gathering in Summer Road in Edgbaston on 12 August 1962. Whilst there he had gone outside with another man to show him his motorbike and that whilst outside they found a naked child in the street and Augustine Dooley said to another child, 'Go and tell your mother to get some clothes on the little one'.

However, a woman then came out and started shouting and using abusive language and she pushed Augustine Dooley and he fell and hit his head on the pavement.

Augustine Dooley then went in.

Augustine Dooley's brother said that later on Augustine Dooley answered the door bell and found the woman's husband there and that he went out with him. He said that a few minutes later, realising there was trouble, he went out himself and saw the woman's husband shaking

Augustine Dooley against a wall and saw his head strike it.

After that, Augustine Dooley's brother drove Augustine Dooley and his wife home, however, the following Friday Augustine Dooley became ill after driving to Birmingham again and died from haemorrhage after head injuries.

When the police spoke to the woman, she said that when she had approached Augustine Dooley that he had told her to get the child dressed and called her a slut and that she had pushed him in the chest and that he had staggered back and fallen.

She said that her son was only two years old and was always taking his trousers off.

The woman's husband said that when his wife told him what had happened that he had gone next door intending to ask for an apology, but that Augustine Dooley had become aggressive and he had defended himself.

At the inquest, the Coroner noted that there had been a break in the chain of circumstantial evidence about how Augustine Dooley received his fatal injuries, further noting that it was possible that Augustine Dooley had fallen from his machine during his second visit to Birmingham and hurt himself and had not told anybody.

An open verdict was returned.

Baby

Age: 0

Sex: female

Date: 7 Sep 1962

Place: Hill Top, West Bromwich

The body of a newly-born female child was found dead in a paper carrier bag on the canal side at Hill Top on Saturday 1 September 1962.

It was found to have been stabbed 30 times. All the wounds were said to have been caused by the same instrument. In one place the brain had been penetrated.

The pathologist said that he thought that it was possible that the wounds could have been caused by a thin knife with a double cutting edge. He said:

It could have been a nail file or a small Commando type knife.

The police said that they were making enquiries but that nothing had come to light so far that would be helpful. However, they said that they were certain that someone could give them information if they wished, saying:

Someone obviously knows who the mother of this baby is.

The body of another female child was found in the canal at Hill Top in West Bromwich the previous year on 10

April 1961, although its cause of death was given as being due to asphyxia at birth.

New Born Girl

Age: 0

Sex: female

Date: 1 Sep 1962

Place: Staffordshire

The body of a newly born girl was found in Staffordshire

The details were reported in the Staffordshire Constabularies Homicide Return, which stated:

Despite all possible enquiries the mother of this newly born child has not been traced and no information concerning the circumstances under which it was murdered have been obtained.

An inquest was held at the Law Courts, West Bromwich, on 26 February, 1963, by the coroner sitting with a jury. A verdict of Murder by some person or persons unknown was returned.

Wesley Spencer McCallum

Age: 28

Sex: male

Date: 2 Aug 1962

Place: unknown

Wesley Spencer McCallum was stabbed outside 3 Cromer Road in Eastville, Bristol on the night of Thursday 2 August 1962.

A man was tried for his murder but acquitted. He claimed he had acted in self-defence.

The court heard that the man tried had been at loggerheads with another man over a girl and that on the night of 2 August 1962 they had had a row over it outside 3 Cromer Road during which the accused man stabbed Wesley McCallum and two other men.

He initially denied having stabbed Wesley McCallum but at his trial he claimed that he had acted in self-defence.

The knife used to kill Wesley McCallum was found at the scene and the court heard that it was later shown to have belonged to the man tried.

The Accused Man

The accused man said that he first met the woman concerned about three months earlier when he moved into 1 Napier Road in Eastville and soon after started to have sexual intercourse with her, noting that she told him that she had also been having sexual intercourse with another man, a labourer who was one of the men later involved in the stabbing outside 3 Cromer Road in which Wesley McCallum died.

He said that around June 1962 that the woman told him that she wanted to finish with the labourer because he was married and that if he came to the house that he was not to take any notice of him. However, he said that the following day that the woman said:

The labourer is good to me. I cannot give him up. You must hide and come to me when he is at work.

The accused man noted that he and the labourer worked at the same place but had been on different shifts. He said that he didn't like what the woman told him and told her that he was going to finish with her and he left 1 Napier Road and went to live at 5 Brenner Street. However, he said that after that the woman sometimes came to visit him and he went to see her.

He said that up until that time he had been paying the woman £3 a week. However, he later said to her:

This is no good you do not cook for me and you live a prostitute life. I would rather put a ring on a pig woman rather than have a prostitute for a wife. I will give you a record as a parting gift.

He said that he bought a record called 'I will', and took it round to her at 1 Napier Road. However, he said the landlady was there and that she stopped him walking up to her room and called the woman to come down and see him. He said that when the woman came down she told him that she had a man up in her room but that he had come to see the landlady but could not go to her room as her children were there and they would tell the landladies husband.

The accused man said that he then gave the record to the woman and left.

He said the following day that the woman and the landlady stopped him in the street and told him that he was jealous and foolish and that he replied:

I don't mind. I am not coming back.

He said that the following week that he went to bingo at the Odeon in Bedminster and met the landlord from 1 Napier Road, the woman, and a man that also lived at 1 Napier Road. He said that the other man had a car and that he afterwards drove them all back to Napier Road and that when he went in he saw the labourer sitting in the hall and said hello to him. He said that the labourer replied:

You must not fuck around here.

He said that he told him that he was ignorant and that the woman then went up to her room followed by the labourer. However, he said that he then went up to the woman's room to make peace with the labourer but said that he came out of the room at him with a knife and told him not to fuck around there. He said that the landlady then told him not to pay him any mind and took him downstairs and the other man then drove him home to 3 Cromer Road, where he was living by that time.

He said that in mid July 1962, on a Saturday, that he went to the bingo again and that when he came out he saw the woman and her landlord by the bus stop. He said the landlord said hello to him and that the woman then asked him why he sent a message to her via a coloured man that lived off Seymour Road who was a friend of hers. He said that he had a lot of records and that one day he found one that didn't belong to him and noted that he had lent the woman some records and that she had returned them two short, but that he later found one amongst them that was not his and thought that it might have been the woman's and so sent the message to enquire whether it was hers.

However, he said that the woman replied:

You must not send any messages to me. I am going to set a trap for you in your house. If you don't get it in your breakfast plate it will be on your dinner plate. I am going to poison you because you can't stop me coming to the house.

However, the accused man said that he replied:

Chink and dog fleas are the worst. They never show up until they go in crowds. If I put myself on a fowl roost, I must expect filth to fall on me.

He said that he then told her that she was the worst girl that he had ever put himself with and that she asked him, 'What about the other girl', the other girl being the wife of a man that lived at 24 Walton Street, noting that he had been with her and then saying that she was going to tell her husband and that he would put a gang onto him.

The accused man noted that the man at 24 Walton Street came from the same district in Jamaica as Wesley

McCallum, the labourer and his landlord at 3 Cromer Road and that he was the only stranger amongst them, they coming from Hanover and he coming from St Thomas.

He said that when the bus came that he went upstairs and the woman and her landlord sat downstairs and that he didn't see them again.

He said he went to bingo again on Saturday night, 28 July 1962, and that on his way home the man from 24 Walton Street stopped him and told him that he was going to put a gang on him because he had been boasting about going with his wife, adding that the woman had told him. However, he said that he told him that he couldn't hurt him and denied having been with his wife and turned away and left.

He said that on Sunday night, 29 July 1962 that he went to bingo again and met the woman and her landlord as they were coming out by the bus stop and told the woman that the man from 24 Walton Street had told him that she had told him that he had gone with his wife and that she was setting on him and that he would go to the police about it so that they could not hurt him.

He said that the following morning he went to Eastville police station about mid-day and told them that he had been threatened, but said that they told him that they could not take a note of all things like that else they would fill their book, and told him that if a gang was raised against him that he was to get a witness.

He said that nothing happened after that until the night of 2 August 1962. He said that he worked during the day from 7.30am to 7.30pm and left work with a friend and went to a pub on Days Road where they each had two bottles of Guinness. He said that he later left his friend in the pub and went looking for a room as he didn't feel safe at 3 Cromer Road and later got back home at 9.30pm because he didn't have a front light on his bicycle and left it there beneath the front window and then went off again looking for a room around St Pauls.

He said that he thought he got back to 3 Cromer Road about 11.30pm at which time he saw a white car on the opposite side of the road with two coloured men sitting in it.

He said that before going in he looked through the front window and saw the landlord and landlady there along with the labourer and Wesley McCallum. He said that when he went in that he went straight up to his room and looked at a bill. He said that his door was open and he could see down the stairs and saw the people going out. He said that about five minutes later he went out and put his bike in the passage and then went back to shut the door.

He said that when he got there Wesley McCallum asked him who he was and then asked:

What did you tell the landlord at 1 Napier Road about you seeing me in his room?

To which the accused man said he replied:

What are you on about. If you want to tell me something tell me something.

However, he said that the labourer said, 'Don't go no fucking argument with him' and that they both grabbed him and dragged him outside on to the pavement at which point the two men in the car got out and joined them.

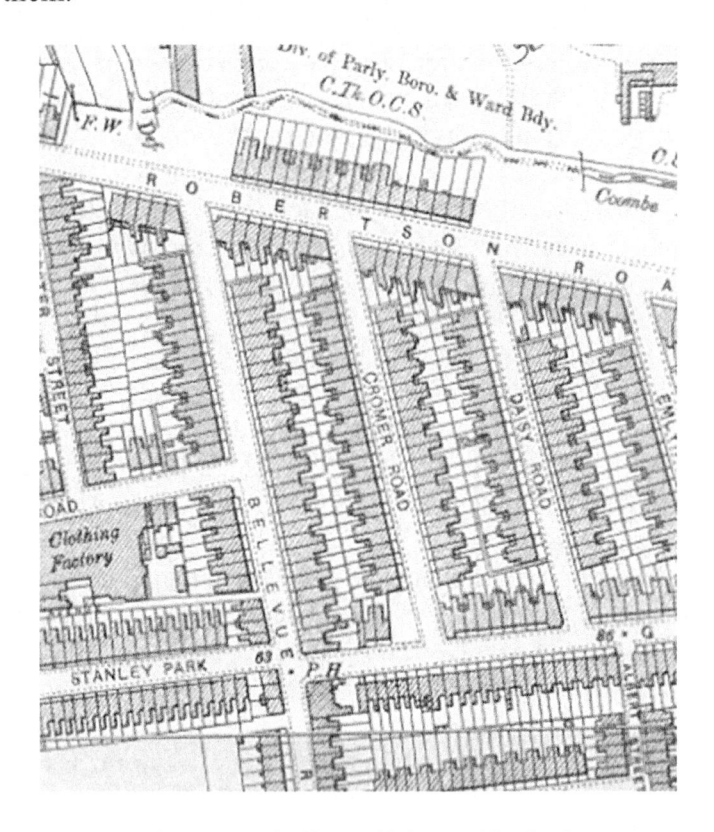

Cromer Road – National Library of Scotland

He said that the landlord then rushed out and pushed him, but thought he did that to protect him. He said that he was then on his knees in a crouching position with his hand up to protect his face when one of the men, who had a knife, brought it down towards his face and that he grabbed the blade and felt a burning in his hand and that he then crawled away and ran off towards Greenbank Road without looking back.

He said that he then ran off towards Eastville police station and that when he got there he saw his landlord who told him:

You have killed a man.

To which he replied:

I know nothing about it.

In his statement to the police he said that he didn't use a knife at all, that the knife he was shown was not his, and that he didn't carry a knife.

When he was seen at the Bristol Royal Infirmary, he said:

When I went home tonight there was four men waiting for me. They started to flash knives around. The landlord of my place got between them and me and he pushed me down on the ground. I crawled away and ran down to the police station. They were all friends. They come from the same district in Jamaica. I've been with a girl who comes from 1 Napier Road, I tell her that before I put ring on her finger I put it on a pig. She living prostitute life. She came from same district as others in Jamaica. The labourer is one of the men who are friends. They say they going to poison me. They all come from the same parish in Jamaica. I the only stranger in the house.

The policeman that saw him then told him that Wesley McCallum was dead and that two others were seriously injured.

At his trial, it was heard that the knife had been his and he claimed he acted in self-defence.

Labourer

When the labourer, who worked at St Annes Board Mills gave evidence he said that he had known the accused man since April 1962 and had also known the woman who lived at 1 Napier Road.

He said that he remembered visiting the woman at 1 Napier Road one night and finding the accused man sat there, but said he didn't say anything to him.

He said that on another occasion he had been sitting in the hall at 1 Napier Road when the accused man came in on his own, followed soon after by the woman. He said the accused man said good afternoon to him but that he replied:

I don't want no how d'you do from you.

To which he said the accused man took him by the shoulder and said:

What are you going on with?

He said that he then went upstairs to the woman's room and sat down but said that the accused man then came in and shook him and said to him:

I'm not keeping up no argument with you.

He said that when the accused man shook him he saw that he had a knife in his hand, noting that it wasn't a penknife, but was a long knife with a fixed blade that wouldn't shut. He said that the woman then pushed him down the stairs and the landlord took him out of the house.

He said that on the night of 2 August 1962 that he had been in the Black Swan public house in Eastville with Wesley McCallum, his brother and another man and a while later the landlord from 3 Cromer Road came in and joined their party.

He said that they left the pub at closing time, around 10.30pm to 10.45pm and all went off in Wesley McCallum's brother's car to 3 Cromer Road, parking outside at the gate and went inside into the front room on the ground floor. He said the landlord fetched his wife down and the others all had a drink, but he didn't.

He said that he didn't know what time they left, but said that they all had a good time. He said that Wesley McCallum's brother and the other man were the first to leave and that they went out and sat outside in the car. He said that as he left he looked up the stairs and saw the accused man sitting in his bedroom at the top of the stairs, but said that they didn't speak to each other and that he then walked out of the house.

He said that the car was on the other side of the road and that the two other friends were sat in it and that he then got in the back seat. He said that whilst he was sitting in the car that he looked out of the window and saw the accused man standing by the gate with his hands in his trouser pockets. He said that Wesley McCallum then came out and that he saw him and the accused man talking and arguing, and then heard the accused man say to Wesley McCallum:

Why are you fucking around with my name for?

He said that he heard nothing before that, but then heard Wesley McCallum say:

You carried my name to the landlord.

And then heard him tell the accused man that he mustn't put him in trouble or fool around with his name any more. He said that he then heard the accused man tell Wesley McCallum that he had been waiting a long time for him.

He said that he then saw the accused man put his right hand by his side, but didn't see what he took from his pocket. He said that they then started to fight and that he got out of the car and then saw that Wesley McCallum was bleeding from the nose. He said that he then asked:

What did you stab Mr McCullum for?

He noted that he hadn't seen any stabbing, but saw him bleeding through his nose.

He said that as he said that that Wesley McCallum hit the accused man with his fist and that the accused man dropped in front of him and he hit him twice about the ear.

However, he said that the accused man then stooped down and stabbed him twice under his left arm. He said that he then grabbed his arm where he had been stabbed and that the accused man then grabbed him and cut him in his tummy from his arm to his navel, but didn't see what he cut him with.

He said that after he cut him that he stood there and saw the accused man walking around looking at the ground whilst Wesley McCallum was walking up and down and moving his head up and down.

He said that he then saw the accused man take a knife out of his hip pocket and was about to open it when he kicked out at him and he dropped the knife in front of him and jumped by the wall. He said that he then picked up the knife, but had no idea what it was like. He noted that he didn't own a knife and didn't have a knife on him that night.

He said that after he picked up the knife that the accused man ran off up Cromer Road.

He said that he then went to go into 3 Cromer Road but fainted at the door, noting that he was carrying the knife when he fainted.

The police later recovered two knives, later labelled exhibits 3 and 4.

Woman

The woman that lived at 1 Napier Road in Eastville said that she knew the accused man when he had lodged at 1 Napier Road, but said that he left thereabout May 1962 although he sometimes returned to collect letters. She said that on one time he called and asked her to come and live with him but told him that she was going to do that and that he told her that her people had told her to say that, adding that if he didn't catch her one way, that he would catch her another.

She said that she remembered returning from bingo one Friday or Saturday evening with her landlord and another man to find the accused man outside. She said that she went into the house and saw the labourer there in the hall and then went up to her room with the labourer, who sat in a chair. She said that the accused man then also came up and stood outside the door, which was open, but didn't hear what he said. However, she said that she heard the labourer say, 'I'm not having any argument with you'. She said that the accused man was standing there with his two hands in his pockets and that she said to him:

You're not to come here making a fuss because you don't live here.

She said that the accused man then went downstairs and nothing more was said.

She said that on another occasion when she was out at the bingo with her landlord that she met the accused man outside at the door to the Odean cinema and he said:

Has your people told you not to come and stay with me? If I don't catch you one way, I'll catch you another. If I don't catch you I must catch somebody for you. I have a knife here ready for anyone.

She said that nothing more was said after that.

She noted that she had seen him with a knife before which she stated was similar to exhibit 3 and that the last time she saw him with a knife was when he lived at Napier Road. She added that she had also seen him with a pocket knife, similar to exhibit 4.

Landlord at 3 Cromer Road

The landlord at 3 Cromer Road said that he was a carpenter and lived there with his wife. He said that the accused man had occupied a bed-sitting room at his house since the beginning of July 1962, his room being on the first floor at the top of the stairs, overlooking the staircase and the front door.

He said that the accused man came into his room on the Sunday whilst he was there with his wife and that he told his wife that the labourer was going to make up a gang to fight him and that if they came to fight him somebody was going to be sorry, and that he said to him:

You mustn't take no notice.

He said that on the night of Thursday 2 August 1962 that he went to the Grosvenor public house and then went on by bus to the Black Swan public house at Eastville where he met some friends, including Wesley McCallum and his brother, the labourer and a fourth man with whom he had some drinks.

He said that they all left at about 10.30pm and went back to his house in Wesley McCallum's brother's car and had some drinks in his front room which he provided.

He said that they later left at about something to twelve, Wesley McCallum's brother and the fourth man going first, followed by the labourer and that he spent a few minutes talking to Wesley McCallum in the passage.

He said that Wesley McCallum then went outside and he went out to say goodbye and that he then saw the accused man with his hands in his pockets.

He said that Wesley McCallum then said to the accused man:

I understand you are talking lying stories on me. I'm a man who doesn't interfere in other people's business.

He said that the labourer had been over the other side of the road at the time, but that he then came over and all three of them were talking.

He said that after Wesley McCallum spoke to the accused man that the accused man replied:

You can say anything you want to say.

He said that they then all started rowing and that Wesley McCallum said:

You're telling him on me and I don't like it.

He said that the accused man then moved his hand across near the three of them and that he intervened because they were getting rough and that both Wesley McCallum and the accused man swore and cursed. He then told them that he didn't want any brawling there, noting that he didn't see anything in the accused man's hand, however, he said that as he moved his hands he brushed against him and he felt a slight pain in his left side.

He said that the accused man then ran up towards Greenbank and Wesley McCallum went after him a few yards and then came back and said something to him and then fell to the ground. He noted that the labourer was also there 'spinning around' in the street.

He noted that he didn't see any blows, just the sideways movement of his hands.

He said that he then ran to Eastville police station and spoke to an officer on duty there and saw blood on his shirt. He said that whilst he was talking to the officer there that the accused man came in and that when he came up, he said:

This is the man that did the cutting.

He said that the accused man then said:

They ganged me.

However, the landlord of 3 Cromer Road said:

That's a lie. Some friends came to look for me and it was no gang.

The accused man was tried at the Bristol Assizes but acquitted on Friday 16 November 1962. He was also acquitted of four other counts of wounding relating to the wounds caused to the labourer and the landlord after the prosecution offered no evidence.

The defence stated that it only needed a spark to set them alight. The defence noted that Wesley McCallum believed that the accused man had been speaking about an alleged affair with another man's wife and that the labourer had no love for him because of their joint association with the woman from 1 Napier Road. The defence said that the situation was of:

These two men going for the accused and the accused really believing that his life was in danger and lashing out in desperation to keep these people at bay.

The prosecution said that the principle question was whether the accused caused the death of Wesley McCallum, noting that there was no doubt that the wound was caused by a knife and that they now knew that that knife had belonged to the accused. The prosecution referred to what he termed the accused's:

Combination of defending himself against attack, coupled with some degree of provocation.

The defence summed up by saying:

You may think that a fair view was that in the heat of the moment, after high words had been spoken and blows struck, this man, instead of running away, took that knife out of his pocket, opened it, and struck recklessly and wildly at the people he was fighting.

It was in that light suggested that a fair verdict would be manslaughter and not murder.

However, after the judge summed up for 2½ hours, the jury found the accused man not guilty.

Geffrey Bacon

Age: 44

Sex: male

Date: 1 Aug 1962

Place: Porton Down

Geffrey Bacon died from pneumonic plague on Wednesday 1 August 1962.

He had worked at the germ-war facility at Porton Down. He had been a senior experimental officer at the Microbiological Research Establishment for the previous fourteen years. His job was to study the cross-breeding of germs and how one generation of germs differed from another.

It was said that he had handled deadly germs at the facility, including smallpox and the plague.

He died following a sudden two day illness. It was thought that he might have picked up a germ whilst at his work. It was initially reported that it was thought he had died from a disease so rare that the doctors didn't even know if it was infectious.

His wife said:

The hospital said he died of pneumonia, though it seems they don't know what caused it.

It was reported that a scientist at the research facility said:

It is a complete mystery at the moment. Tests which may show the cause of death will take at least 24 hours.

It was added that precautions were limited until it was known what germ might have caused his death.

It was said that in the weeks before his death that he had been handling germs, most of them being harmless, in his own laboratory and in the section where experimental animals were housed.

He had lived at Hop Gardens, Whiteparish, near Salisbury and had two daughters.

A war office spokesman said that Geffrey Bacon died:

in circumstances which make it possible that death was due to an accidental infection resulting from his work at the establishment.

The War Office were reported to have emphasised that research at Porton Down was only into 'defensive measures' against biological warfare. It was stated that extraordinary safety precautions were taken at the facility and that every corner of the laboratories, hidden among farmlands behind red 'danger' notices, were regularly searched for stray germs, it being added that all the air and water was filtered before it left the building.

It was said that scientists handling the most dangerous germs used breathing masks and protective clothing and had a shower and changed their clothes completely before leaving. It was also noted that there was a ban on leaving litter, even toffee papers, about, in case they harboured strange germs.

It was also noted that staff at the facility were inoculated against up to ten diseases, and that their families were often also protected.

The director of the establishment said:

There is no positive reason to suppose that Mr Bacon died of any disease which he contacted through his work with us. But we are carrying out full investigations because all personnel in an establishment of this kind run the risk of being infected with the organisms with which they deal.

Robert Jenkins

Age: 31

Sex: male

Date: 24 Jul 1962

Place: New Bridge Street, Newcastle

Robert Jenkins was stabbed outside a pub on the night of 4 May 1962 in Newcastle.

He died in the ambulance on the way to the hospital.

Several people were tried but were convicted of lesser offences.

They had been drinking in the public house in New Bridge Street, Newcastle and later attacked three men, including Robert Jenkins, knocking them to the ground, with one of them stabbing Robert Jenkins.

They all pleaded guilty to fighting and causing an affray.

When the judge sentenced them, he said:

You made a pretty savage attack on these men. Both were knocked down and repeatedly kicked. Five of you admit kicking him. And as if this was not bad enough, one of you seven must have the crime of murder on you, for Jenkins was stabbed through the heart and died as a result. Then you ran away.

They were all sentenced to 3 years, however, the judge later reduced the sentence on six of the youths to 2 years, stating that it was unfair to treat them all the same as the one that was cleared of murder and who was described as the ring leader.

The convicted youths were:

1. Butcher boy, 17, of Silver Lonon, Newcastle, sentenced to 3 years.
2. Apprentice plumber, 19, of Grasmere Avenue, Newcastle, sentenced to 2 years.
3. Labourer, 20, of Wigmore Avenue, Newcastle, sentenced to 2 years.
4. Labourer, 22, of St Anthony's Road, Newcastle, sentenced to 2 years.
5. Trainee mill operator, 18, of Chatsworth Gardens, Newcastle, sentenced to 2 years.
6. Apprentice joiner, 19, of Pinner Place, Newcastle, sentenced to 2 years.
7. Porter, 24, of Mortimer Avenue, Newbiggen Hall Estate, Westerhope, Newcastle, sentenced to 2 years.

Robert Jenkins had lived at Greenhow Place in Newcastle.

Olive Mary Duncan

Age: 61

Sex: female

Date: 18 Jul 1962

Place: 51 Sulgrave Gardens, Hammersmith

Olive Mary Duncan died after being tied up by an intruder in her flat in Sulgrave Gardens, Hammersmith on 18 July 1962.

She had also been raped. She was found with her wrists tied.

Her inquest heard that she died from acute fear. She was said to have died about 12 minutes after neighbours heard moaning and the breaking of glass coming from her flat around midnight

The pathologist said that her death was caused by a waterlogging of the lungs from heart failure caused by an acute emotional crisis, or in other words, 'acute fear'.

At her inquest the Coroner noted that she had been raped, but that she might have been unconscious when that happened, and noted that her death was not directly connected with violence, but was the result of a criminal act. In answer to a question from the Coroner, the pathologist noted that a woman of her age might have accepted the rape rather than struggle.

An open verdict was returned.

Olive Duncan had been a City secretary and insurance clerk.

It was thought that Olive Duncan had been attacked by a man that also attacked two other elderly women in their bedrooms.

The police said that they called in more than 100 plain clothes police to help in the search, which was concentrated in the area between Notting Hill and Hammersmith, where two of the victims lived.

The police said that they knew that the attacker was small, very strong and agile and that they thought that he might have scratches on his face.

Neighbours said that shortly after hearing Olive Duncan scream that they saw a man walking away from the flats.

A caretaker that lived next to Olive Duncan said that she had been a quiet living person and that he had never known men on their own to visit her. He said that about 12.30am on Wednesday 18 July 1962 that his wife wakened him and said that she could hear moaning. He said:

I got up and heard a faint mumbling and then I heard glass breaking. I phoned 999 asking for the police and an ambulance and went out. A window of Miss Duncan's flat was flapping. A neighbour came up and climbed through the window. He opened the front door and let me in.

He said that before he entered the flat that he saw Olive Duncan by the window and noticed that she was a bit puffed in the face and a blue colour. He said that she had apparently put her fist through a pane of glass. He said he saw her raise up her hands and saw that her hands were tied together in front of her by a piece of rag or pillow slip and noted a few spots of blood on it.

He said that when he entered her bedroom that he saw water running down the dressing table mirror as if Olive Duncan had thrown water at someone. He said that the bed was in disorder and that Olive Duncan had been lying half on the floor and half on the bed and trying to pull herself up on her elbows.

He said that she didn't speak and that she died about twelve minutes later whilst he was there.

The man that climbed in through the window said that after hearing a groaning noise he called out, 'Who are you and what number are you?' and got the reply 51. He said that after getting in through the bedroom window that he switched the light on and untied Olive Duncan's hands and she said, 'Thank God' and asked for some water. He said that he then found the key of the front door on the hall stand and unlocked the door and opened it.

In answer to a question from the Coroner at the inquest he said that the nightdress that Olive Duncan had been wearing had been disturbed.

A woman that had an upper flat in Sulgrave Gardens said that she was awakened by the sound of breaking glass and looked out and saw a man turn the corner of the road, but didn't recognise him. She noted that he was walking and not running. She said that there was a lot of disturbance going on and that a neighbour asked her to phone the police.

She said that the man had been there when the second pane of glass was broken, and that there was enough noise to arrest the attention of the ordinary person but that the man didn't turn around.

Another neighbour said that she also saw the man walking away. She said that he had been wearing dark clothes and had had no hat and said that he didn't turn around.

She said that she soon after went into Olive Duncan's flat. She said that Olive Duncan was groaning quite a lot and that she held her in her arms and gave her some water but that she then collapsed.

A detective inspector that had been in charge of the investigation said that 500 statements had been taken and almost 1,000 people interviewed and that they evoked the assistance of police forces throughout the country with the object of tracing the man who was seen to leave the flats after the assault.

He said that a road check had been made in the vicinity to try and trace any person that might have seen the man and that the assistance of the national Press and of the TV companies had been sought.

He said that he had no doubt that the intruder had entered the flat through the top transom window of the toilet and had left through the window in the sitting room.

He noted that there was no conclusive evidence that anything had been stolen from the flat and that he had heard that Olive Duncan had had very little money in the flat and had had a banking account.

The pathologist that carried out the post mortem said that Olive Duncan had slight injuries to her fingers, thigh and neck but that her injuries were really very small and concluded that she had died from water logging of the lungs resulting from heart failure precipitated by acute emotional crisis, that being in other words, fright or fear.

The pathologist agreed that the nervous shock might have caused temporary unconsciousness, and when the Coroner asked:

In the ordinary course of life, such as hurrying for a bus, would you have expected this lady's heart to have been such as to have caused sudden death?

The pathologist replied, 'No'.

When the Coroner summed up he noted that Olive Duncan had lived in Sulgrave Gardens for about three years and had been a lady of the most highly respected character.

The three women attacked were:

1. 61-year-old Olive Duncan, Sulgrave Gardens, Hammersmith, July 1962.
2. Woman from Nottinghill who asked for her identity to be kept secret.
3. 70-year-old housewife, Nottinghill, Saturday 24 November 1962.

The 70-year-old housewife had fought off her attacker and scratched his face.

It was also thought that other elderly women had been attacked in their bedrooms but that they had been too afraid to come forward.

The police appealed for landladies and hotel owners in the Hammersmith and Nottinghaill areas to tell the police if they had any lodgers or guests with scratches on their face.

John McDonald

Age: 18

Sex: male

Date: 15 Jul 1962

Place: Cathkin Hotel, East Kilbride Road, Burnside, Lanarkshire

John McDonald was stabbed in the forecourt of the Cathkin Hotel in East Kilbride Road, Burnside, Lanarkshire on 15 July 1962.

A man was tried for his murder but acquitted.

The judge noted that it was clear from the evidence that not all the witnesses were telling the truth, although he noted that 'It may be that few of them are telling very much of the truth'.

John McDonald had lived in Caledonian Circuit, Cambuslang.

Baby

Age: 0

Sex: male

Date: 29 Jun 1962

Place: Gainsford Place, Islington

The body of a newly-born female child was found at a house in Gainsford Place, Islington.

An inquest at St Pancras heard that it died from unascertained causes.

Nothing more is known.

George Bailey

Age: 22

Sex: male

Date: 9 Jun 1962

Place: All Saints Tavern, 103 York Street, Manchester

George Bailey died following an assault at a public house.

He was found unconscious outside the All Saints Tavern in York Street, Manchester on Friday 8 June 1962. He was found spawled out on his back on the pavement with a cut to the back of his head.

He was taken to hospital where it was reported that he was 'brought back from the dead', but died 17 hours later. His heart had stopped beating when he arrived at the hospital, but doctors used the 'kiss of life' method of resuscitation and massaged his heart, to restore his breathing and he was then put in an oxygen tent.

He had lived in Alexandra Place, Collyhurst in Manchester and had been a waiter in a Manchester restaurant.

It was noted that on the day he died that he should have been going on holiday.

All Saints Tavern, 103 York Street, Manchester – Manchester Libraries

John McGourty

Age: 61

Sex: male

Date: 6 Jun 1962

Place: The Fountain, 74 St Georges Road, London, SE1

John McGourty was battered to death at a derelict public house on 6 June 1962 at about 3.10am.

The public house had been The Fountain at 74 St George's Road, London. Following the attack, he was taken to Lambeth Hospital where he died two hours later.

John McGourty was described as an elderly and shabby tramp.

It was thought that he had been kicked to death by a gang of teenage youths for fun. He died before he could tell the police anything, however, his companion, who was also beaten, gave evidence of what he described as a night of terror.

It was said that John McGourty had been thrust through a door in the room that he had been sleeping in in the building and kicked and punched.

At his inquest in Southwark on 8 August 1962 the Coroner appealed for witnesses to help the police trace the murderers, saying:

Quite a lot of people must have some knowledge that these youths were involved in this so-called sport. These people are protecting a group of young sadists. I hope, arising out of the publicity this case will get, someone will go forward to the police.

When the Coroner addressed the jury he said that the only possible verdict was murder, adding:

You may well think this shows a degree of bestiality and sadism which we don't like to believe is present in English youth. This gang has attacked these old tramps for pure sadism.

John McGourty's companion's statement stated that they had been sleeping in the derelict public house in St George's Road, Southwark, John McGourty being in the room below him, when he was awakened by young Cockney voices and the sounds of a fight below. He said that when he realised what was happening that he got down in a corner and pulled his coat over him, hoping they wouldn't find him, but that a few minutes later five or six boys came into the room and one said, 'Theres another tramp over there'.

He said that they dragged him across the room and kicked him and that someone knelt on him and he was then struck on the head with a brick.

He said that the youth's then left him and went to the stairs, but that one of them said:

Let's give him some more.

And that they returned to kick him again.

He said that he eventually staggered downstairs where he was found by a police officer who later found John McGourty dying from brain injuries.

Forty-seven youths were interviewed following his murder. However, the police said:

But the latest we could get anyone being near the public house was 1.50am. We have succeeded in finding three independent persons who live near the public house, and they each saw three young men walking away from the direction of the public house at about the material time.

The pathologist said that John McGourty's death was due to contusion of the brain and haemorrhage. He said that there was a fracture of the check bone and fractures of four ribs and marks on his neck compatible with the pinning of his neck by someone's fingers.

He said there was deep bruising on the stomach as though made by someone kneeling on him, and that injuries down his left side were compatible with him having been thrust through a door.

The Coroner added:

This seems to be a gang of young thugs who have taken pleasure in beating up harmless tramps.

The inquest returned a verdict of murder by a person or persons unknown.

Baby

Age: 0

Sex: male

Date: 5 Jun 1962

Place: White Post Hill, Redhill, Surrey

The body of a newly-born male child was found in a shallow grave on the common land in Redhill on 5 June 1962.

The cause of death was head injuries and it had superficial bruising on its forehead.

It was found on common land near White Post Hill.

An inquest was held at Reigate on 15 June 1962, where the jury returned a verdict of murder by some person or persons unknown.

No further developments were made.

It was noted that another child's body was found 200 yards away in May 1962 and it was considered that they were almost certainly connected crimes, but were recorded as separate crimes as there was no positive evidence to connect the two.

White Post Hill, Redhill – National Library of Scotland

Baby

Age: 0

Sex: male

Date: 17 May 1962

Place: White Post Hill, Redhill, Surrey

The body of a newly-born male child was found in a shallow grave in the common near White Post Hill at Redhill on 17 May 1962.

It was found at 7.30pm.

It was found to have superficial bruising on its forehead.

The cause of death was given as a fractured skull, and the inquest, held on 13 June 1962, returned an open verdict.

It was noted that another child's body was found 200 yards away in June 1962 and it was considered that they were almost certainly connected crimes, but were recorded as separate crimes as there was no positive evidence to connect the two.

Baby

Age: 0

Sex: male

Date: 29 Apr 1962

Place: Surrey

The body of a newly-born male child was found on common land in Surrey.

The child had been asphyxiated.

The child's inquest on 25 May 1962 was held at Woking and an open verdict was returned.

Michael James Reynolds

Age: 22

Sex: male

Date: 26 Apr 1962

Place: Chalfont St Peter

Michael James Reynolds was found injured in the road at Chalfont St Peter on the night of 26 April 1962.

He was taken to Amersham Hospital but pronounced dead on arrival.

He had lived in Shephard's Bush but had been a former patient at Chalfont Epileptic Colony and had been there for a visit.

The night attendant at the colony said that when Michael Reynolds left at 9.30pm to catch a bus that he appeared to be quite well.

The pathologist that carried out the post mortem said that Michael Reynolds had been healthy and that there were no signs of disease. Describing his severe head injuries, he said, 'I thought they were consistent with having been struck by some kind of blunt instrument. I found very little else. There were no injuries to the body, which puzzled me. One theory is that, if he was struck while standing up, he could have been leaning forward so that his head was ahead of his body.

When the Coroner at the inquest addressed the jury, he said, 'The question is, how did he come by his injuries? A most likely theory seems to be that he was struck while crossing the road by some fast-moving vehicle, or, possibly, he stumbled into the path of a car. But of course, all this is guesswork'.

The jury then returned an open verdict.

His death was described as a road death mystery.

Laurel Barrett

Age: 31

Sex: female

Date: 18 Apr 1962

Place: 91 Pepys Road, New Cross

Laurel Barrett died following an abortion.

It was found that there had been instrumental interference, but it could not be determined by who.

She had been living at 91 Pepys Road in New Cross.

A friend of hers, a 29-year-old woman who lived in Landcroft Road, East Dulwich, said that they had been friends and that she knew of the pregnancy, but knew nothing about an illegal operation.

An open verdict was returned.

Winifred Williams

Age: 32

Sex: female

Date: 8 Apr 1962

Place: 17 Meeting House Lane, Peckham

Winifred Williams died from an attempted abortion, however it was not possible to state whether it was self-inflicted or whether any third party had been involved.

She had been a coloured woman.

When the police searched her room at 17 Meeting House Lane in Peckham they found a syringe.

She had previously stayed at a house in Leytonstone with her two-year-old boy but had been asked to leave by the landlord who said:

I gave her a month's notice in October as I found out about her boyfriend staying all night. I have reason to suspect that he even had a key.

He said that she had been very friendly with another tenant who would occasionally spend the night with her.

Of the woman's death, the landlord said:

At midnight I heard a thumping on the wall. I rushed upstairs thinking something had happened to her child, and found her dead. I noticed a strong peppermint smell, the same smell which existed when she was living here before.

Jacqueline Boyle

Age: 18 months

Sex: male

Date: 1 Apr 1962

Place: Philbeach Convalescent Home, Station Road, Hythe

Jacqueline Boyle died in a fire at the Philbeach Convalescent Home in Station Road, Hythe on 1 April 1962.

However, it wasn't known how the fire started. A box of matches was later found between the folds and feathers of the damp mattress.

Jacqueline Boyle had been asleep in a cot in room 15 at the time.

The Coroner said that the fire could have been started in one of three ways.

1. Somebody went into the room to have a look at Jacqueline Boyle while smoking a cigarette and the end dropped off into the bedding.
2. Jacqueline Boyle might have had a box of matches in the bed that she had picked up.
3. Someone had deliberately set fire to the cot.

Bertha Davies

Age: 56

Sex: female

Date: 27 Mar 1962

Place: Queen Street, Oldbury

Bertha Davies was found dead on some waste ground near Oldbury town centre on 27 March 1962.

She was found by a man that had lived only a few yards away at back of 13 Queen Street. He said that he saw her body with her clothing disarranged.

She had been wearing a red raincoat.

Bertha Davies had lived in Tonks Street in Oldbury.

A pathologist said that her cause of death was an injury to her head. He said that his examination showed an extensive area of bruising on the left side of her forehead that was not caused by a rough or jagged instrument, but which was consistent with having been made by a fist, with quite a considerable amount of force having been used.

The pathologist added that he thought that Bertha Davies was more likely to have been hit where she was found rather than to have walked there after being hit or to have been carried there.

He also told the Coroner:

To hit a woman on the head with his fist is not a thing which a reasonable man would expect to cause death.

An Indian man that had lived in Queen Street at the time, close to where the body was found, said that he had been with Bertha Davies and some other Indians in a public house on the night of 26 March 1962 after which he, Bertha Davies and another Indian went back to Queen Street where Bertha Davies had more to drink. However, he said she became abusive and was told to go home but that she wouldn't go and that the other Indian man pushed her out. However, he said that as far as he could recall she received no blows.

He added:

She was very drunk when she left the house.

The Coroner then noted to the jury:

You have no evidence of how the blow was sustained. There is no evidence that the other Indian man gave the blow.

A woman that had lived in Portway Road, Oakham, said that she saw a woman in a red coat in Wesley Street, Oldbury, with an Indian. She said:

She kept stopping as if she did not want to go and he kept pulling her.

A man that lived in the same house as Bertha Davies said that she had had a number of blackouts, resulting in her falling down in a faint, noting that he thought drinking had caused the backouts.

Her inquest returned an open verdict.

William Johnstone

Age: 54

Sex: male

Date: 13 Mar 1962

Place: Newington, Annan, Dumfries

William Johnstone was found dead in a disused railway cutting behind his home early on Tuesday 13 March 1962.

He had lived at 7 Fernlea Crescent in Newington, Annan.

He had been a painter.

His death was initially described as a suspected murder, but nothing more is known.

Purnesh Chandra Paul

Age: 29

Sex: male

Date: 11 Mar 1962

Place: Langdon Road, Bromley, Kent

Purnesh Chandra Paul died in his bed.

He had marks on his neck suggesting he had been assaulted, with his death caused by a violent blow.

He was heard groaning in his bed on Sunday night. It was not possible to wake him and he died with a doctor in attendance at his home.

He had been an Indian.

Billy Holloway

Age: 10

Sex: male

Date: 10 Mar 1962

Place: Grand Union Canal, Station Road Bridge, Hayes

Billy Holloway was found drowned in the Grand Union Canal at Hayes on Wednesday 14 March 1962.

He was found in the canal near Station Road Bridge in Hayes about 50 yards from where he was last seen.

The pathologist said that his death was due to drowning and that his body had been in the water for about a month. He had other injuries which were initially thought could have been caused before his death.

He was last seen whilst playing with an 11-year-old friend in Clayton Road in Hayes at the car park by Hayes railway station.

His friend said that shortly before he vanished that he had seen him speaking to a man. Billy Holloway had been missing since Wednesday 14 February 1962.

He had lived at Wheately Crescent in Hayes and had been a Wolf Cub. His father had been a paint sprayer.

He was said to have walked off with a tall thin-faced strange man wearing a fawn raincoat who spoke to him in a car park. Billy Holloway's friend described the thin-faced man to the police. He said that they had been playing at smashing milk bottles and that the man had told them he was a detective and was taking Billy Holloway to the police station.

He said that they had been breaking milk bottles against a wall when the man, 'who said he was a private eye', asked them for their names and addresses and then told him to go home. He said 'I turned round to look back. They were moving away. Billy was walking at the side of the man'. He added that he thought they were going to the police station.

Billy Holloway had been wearing his Cub uniform when he went missing, and it was noted that the cap he had been wearing had not been his own and that the name inside of it had been that of another boy and that in addition to the normal Cub's badge on the cap there was one star.

Before his body was found dead in the canal, a large search was made for him and the police said that they thought that he might be locked in a room or in a shed or garage somewhere and residents were asked to look through their houses to make sure that he was not there unknown to them.

Intensive searches of all open spaces in the area were also made and more than 1,000 volunteers joined in.

Fifty detectives with photos of Billy Holloway questioned people in the area and police in a squad car made loud hailer appeals to anyone who could help.

On Monday 19 February 1962 it was reported that the search was extended towards Cranford Park. A cabbage field was also searched.

A search of the Grand Union Canal was made on 19 February 1962 and it was reported that shop and office workers had crowded on to the bridge over the canal in Hayes High Street during their lunch break to watch a team of Berkshire police frogmen who were taking part in the hunt. It was reported that the frogmen were making constant dives to search the part of the canal that ran through the centre of the town.

Two Hayes boys came forward to say that a man with black, wavy hair and a long face offered them orangeade in a cafe in Uxbridge, adding that he left when they told him to leave them alone.

The police also checked on an ex-prisoner who had a history of sexual attacks on young boys who lived in London.

Watford police also investigated the story of two women who said they saw a lorry driver at a North Watford cafe on the morning of 19 February 1962 with a boy who resembled Billy Holloway. The driver left the cafe before the police arrived, but the woman took the vehicle's number. Two woman that saw the boy said that he had looked 'a bit cold and wary'. They said, 'The boy struck us as having something amiss. The man with him was a typical lorry driver'.

On 19 February 1962 the police also received an anonymous message stating that Billy Holloway could be found 'in Hertfordshire, near the crematorium', after which the police searched the rear of West Herts Crematorium in Garston with tracker dogs.

Billy Holloway's inquest was held in Ealing and returned an open verdict.

The pathologist said that his death was due to drowning and that his body had been in the water for about a month. He said that wounds to his head were typical of injuries caused in waterways where propeller-driven boats passed and that there was nothing to suggest any violence during life.

It was noted by a detective that no evidence was found that would lead to a positive identification of the man referred to by Billy Holloway's 11-year-old friend that was said to have led Billy Holloway away.

The detective added that there was no suspicion of foul play.

Joseph Augustus Hedley

Age: 50

Sex: male

Date: 5 Mar 1962

Place: Coventry

Joseph Augustus Hedley died following a road accident.

An open verdict was returned.

It was heard that the question of whether he died as a result of injuries received in a road accident, or whether his death was from natural causes, was left unanswered.

He had been involved in a road accident whilst riding his cycle on 17 January 1962 and broke his leg. He spent three weeks in hospital and was later released on 6 February. However, on 24 February he began having fits and was readmitted to hospital where he died on 5 March.

His inquest heard that the driver of the car involved in the accident had been prosecuted for careless driving at Coventry Magistrates Court and found guilty.

A consultant pathologist at the Midland centre of neuro-surgery, said that a post mortem examination revealed a clot in the middle cerebral artery. He said that there were no obvious effects upon the brain but that microscopic examinations revealed nerve cell degeneration.

He noted additionally that Joseph Hedley also contracted broncho-pneumonia of the left upper lobe of the lung, which could have developed through him lying in bed with a leg in plaster.

However, he said that his cause of death was lack of blood to the brain due to thrombosis of the middle artery.

He agreed that it was possible that the injuries received in the accident could have caused his death, but added that the clot developed a considerable period after the accident and that he thought his death could have been due to natural causes.

He added that he found no evidence of any injury to his head.

The Coroner noted that it was an unusual case, saying:

Normally after a road accident, the cause of death is only too obvious, but it is not so with this case.

Joseph Hedley had been a Jamaican and had lived at 52 King Edward Road in Coventry.

He had been a labourer with Morris Motors Ltd.

Susan Michelmore

Age: 77

Sex: female

Date: 4 Mar 1962

Place: Burton Street, Brixham, Devon

The body of Susan Michelmore was exhumed after it was thought she might have been poisoned.

She died on 4 March 1962 but was later exhumed on 13 September 1962 after a prisoner in Exeter jail made a statement to the police saying that her death had not been due to natural causes.

She had lived in Burton Street, Brixham and had been widowed three times. At the time of her death she had been crippled with arthritis and bedridden. She was said to have once been a familiar figure in the town, walking about with the aid of crutches to the clifftop to visit friends.

Following her death she was buried at St Mary's churchyard in Brixham.

Her body was exhumed at dawn on the morning of 13 September 1962 in the belief that she might have been poisoned and two scientific experts took away soil samples for tests at the Bristol forensic laboratory.

One of her three sons said that at the time he thought she had died from coronary thrombosis.

At her inquest in November 1962, one of her son's said:

I placed the pillow...

But was stopped by the Coroner who said that it would be better if he said no more.

He was later quoted as having said:

I snuffed my old mother.

When he was questioned by the press, he said:

This matter has worried me because I am not certain whether or not I caused my mother's death.

Adding that he put a pillow over her face when she was in 'agonies of pain'.

The police said that the papers in the case had been placed before the Director of Public Prosecutions, but that no proceedings had taken place.

The inquest concluded that she died from natural causes, coronary thrombosis.

Alan John Vigar

Age: 23

Sex: male

Date: 19 Feb 1962

Place: 29 St Georges Drive, Pimlico, London

Alan John Vigar was found naked with his hands bound behind his back and strangled at his ground floor flat at 29 St Georges Drive in Pimlico on 20 February 1962.

His murder was connected to the murder of Norman Rickard who was found in a similar condition.

He had been a television wardrobe boy for ITV.

He was last seen by a police sergeant who had been in the house next door walking towards his flat with a tall slim man who was said to have had 'classic features' and to have been extraordinarily well dressed.

His inquest returned a verdict of murder by person or persons unknown.

The police sergeant that saw the man earlier with Alan Vigar said that he would recognise the man again. He said that he had been on plain clothes duty on 19 February 1962 sitting in the ground floor front room of 27 St Georges Drive. He said that he had been looking out of a bay window which covered the whole of Warwick Way and could see towards Eccleston Square.

He said that he saw Alan Vigar and the other man come along at about 9.50pm from the direction of Eccleston Square, walking diagonally towards 29 St George's Drive. He said:

St Georges Drive, Pimlico

I had a good look at both of them and took a note of this other man. This other man was about 5ft 10in in height, slim, extraordinarily well-built with fair to blonde hair, clean shaven and he had classic features. I could recognise him again.

The police sergeant then explained that the men passed out of his view and that he didn't see whether they entered 29 St George's Drive. He noted that he had known Alan Vigar for about 12 months but had never spoken to him.

Alan Vigar was found by the resident housekeeper. She said that she had been there for the previous ten years and that Alan Vigar had been there for the previous 18 months. She said that she had found him a 'very nice man indeed' and described him as the best tenant in the house. She noted that she only saw one of his men friends.

When the Coroner asked the housekeeper whether Alan Vigar had ever talked to her about his sexual interests, she replied, 'No, he did not'.

She noted that a lady called for him once but that she thought that it had been his mother.

She added that about two weeks earlier that a man called and left a message for Alan Vigar, but that the man didn't go upstairs. She said that she had never heard any kind of disturbance coming from his room.

She said that she went to his room at about 11.15am on 20 February 1962 to vacuum-clean the carpet and to dust, noting that she knocked at his door, but got no reply, and thought that he had gone out to work as normal, and so she opened the door with a pass key.

She said that when she went in she thought that there was something strange as his bed was not made, noting that he used to make his own bed, and that she found all the bedclothes bunched up together.

She said that she then saw a towel across the top of the bed and felt a bit scared and that when she moved the towel she saw Alan Vigar's face discoloured and pressed down into the pillow and that she could see that he was dead.

She said that she then went downstairs and fetched the owner of the house.

She noted that she didn't notice anything else unusual in the room because she didn't stay there long enough.

She said that the last time she saw Alan Vigar alive was at noon on 19 February 1962 when he left his room. She said that he told her not to bother with his room because he had been away for the weekend. She said that he had been with his friend and had been wearing his camel-hair short coat.

29 St Georges Drive, Pimlico

She explained that her room had been some distance from Alan Vigar's room and that it was separated by a flight of stairs. She said that she had been in her room all that Monday evening and didn't hear a thing, but noted that Alan Vigar had always been very quiet and that she had never previously heard him.

She said that after she told the landlady what she had seen that the police were called.

A police constable said that he received a message whilst in his radio car that there had been an attempted suicide at 29 St George's Drive and that he arrived there with two other officers and an ambulance crew and saw Alan Vigar lying face downwards in the pillow. He added that he noticed a piece of cloth under his neck and a towel under his forehead.

At that stage a detective that had been sitting in the well of the court untied a plastic bag and produced a sleeveless cotton vest, which the police constable said was the piece of cloth he found and put it across his throat to demonstrate how he found it on arrival at the flat.

He said that when he pulled the bedclothes back that he saw that Alan Vigar's hands were tied together behind his back with what appeared to be a dressing gown cord. The dressing gown cord was also produced at the inquest, it being coloured red, blue and yellow.

The police constable noted that the room had been very dark at the time as the electric light had not been working because the plug had not been fixed to switch on the bed-side lamp. However, he noted that the room had been in perfect order and that Alan Vigar's clothes had been neatly folded over the back of two fireside chairs and that there was no indication of there having been a struggle.

The pathologist said that he arrived at the scene at 2.30pm and found that Alan Vigar's left wrist was tied above his right wrist behind his back. He said that he thought that his death had occurred between 1am and 4am, but that if one allowed for a 25% margin that the time could have been between 11pm and 5am.

He said that he found two ligature marks, three quarters of an inch apart round his throat and that he found bloodstains on the pillow, indicating an asphyxial death. He also found some small abrasions on his shoulder that he said could have bene caused by a finger nail.

He said that the post mortem revealed some irregular marks around his throat, the lower one being 7 inches long and the other 6¼ inches long, and suggested that they could have been made by the vest.

The pathologist then demonstrated with the vest, with the assistance of the Coroner's officer, who held up his wrist, how the vest could have been pulled round Alan Vigar's throat like the reins of a horse. He noted that it would not have needed to have been tied to have caused death and that his death had been due to strangulation by a ligature.

When the Coroner asked the pathologist whether he had found anything to suggest a homosexual mode of life, the pathologist replied, 'No, I did not'.

He went on to say that he didn't think that the tying of Alan Vigar's hands could have been done by himself.

When the pathologist was asked whether he thought that the ligature marks could have been self-inflicted, he replied that they could not have been without some elaborate apparatus that would have been found in the room. The Coroner then noted:

In other words these marks must have been inflicted by somebody else.

To which the pathologist replied, 'Yes'.

A man that had lived in Gosberton Road in Balham, said that he had been with Alan Vigar on the eve of his murder. He said that he had been a foreman acetylene burner and had known Alan Vigar for about a year. Before he gave his evidence the Coroner told him that if any questions were asked that he thought might tend to make him consider that he had committed the offence that he had the right not to answer.

The man then said that he had called for Alan Vigar at 9.30am on 19 February 1962 and that they had gone out at 10am to visit a hatter's in Knightsbridge, Victoria and Piccadilly after which they went to a coffee house in the Haymarket. He said that whilst they were at the coffee house that Alan Vigar had wanted to speak privately to a friend and they had parted for five minutes, but that they had been in the coffee house for about an hour.

He said that during the afternoon they strolled around and then went to Knightsbridge before finally parting outside a cinema in Leicester Square.

He said that he tried to telephone Alan Vigar between 7pm and 8pm but that he got no reply.

When he was asked whether Alan Vigar frequently made friends with men that he met in various places, the man replied that Alan Vigar was always interested in meeting people.

When the Coroner asked him, 'From your knowledge of him and, generally speaking, would you say his interest were primarily homosexual?', the man replied, 'No I would not'.

When he was asked, 'Do you think he was interested in women, the man replied, 'Some women'.

When the Coroner suggested, 'If we said he was of homosexual inclination, would that cover it?', the man replied, 'Yes'.

A Grenadier Guardsman said that he had known Alan Vigar for six months and that they had met in some of the clubs in London.

He said that he last saw him alive at 8.20pm on 19 February 1962 at Piccadilly Station and that they had been together there for about three quarters of an hour and that they had gone round the subways to Ward's Irish House and to Leicester Square Station where they parted, noting that they had been walking and talking all the time.

He told the Coroner that he was aware of Alan Vigar's sexual interests. He said that when they parted that Alan Vigar had had some drink but that he was otherwise all right. He said that Alan Vigar had not been worried or frightened and had told him that he was going to meet somebody.

Alan Vigar's brother, a shipping clerk that had lived in Oak Road, Westerham in Kent, said that Alan Vigar visited him in Westerham twice a month and that the last time he saw him was on 18 February 1962.

He said that Alan Vigar used to have the Monday's off and would work Saturdays and Sundays at the television studios.

St Georges Drive, Pimlico

The detective superintendent stated that the cord found at 29 St George's did not belong to either of Alan Vigar's two dressing gowns, but that the vest had been his.

He said that the police had taken 1,000 statements and that 1,500 people had been interrogated. He noted that certain articles of clothing were found to be missing from Alan Vigar's room, including two leather jackets. He added that the only money found was some coppers and that it was possible that some money was also missing. He said that other property found to be missing was an electric razor, a cigarette case and the keys to his room.

When the Coroner summed up at the inquest, he said that the strangulation, if they took into account the tying of the hands and the nature of the marks on his neck, must have been done by somebody else. However, he noted that Alan Vigar must have been a party to the first part of the occurrence.

He said that whilst it was true that a person that had been in the room had carried out the assault on Alan Vigar, that it was far more probable that he had quite willingly submitted to being tied up, possibly in the nature of sexual play, and that the strangulation had been inflicted on him later.

He noted that whether it had been some kind of perverted play that had got out of hand, it was impossible to say.

The jury spent five minutes considering their verdict of murder by a person or persons unknown.

Norman Rickard

Age: 38

Sex: male

Date: 17 Feb 1962

Place: 264A Elgin Avenue, Maida Vale

Norman Rickard was found dead in a wardrobe in his flat at 264A Elgin Avenue, Maida Vale on 19 February 1962.

It was thought he had been murdered on or before 14 February 1962.

He was found naked with his hands bound behind his back and strangled.

His murder was connected to the murder of John Vigar who was found in a similar condition on 20 February 1962.

Norman Rickard had been a civil servant.

The police interviewed 2,000 people and took 400 statements, but the killer was not found.

His inquest was held on Thursday 24 May 1962 at St Pancras where a verdict of murder by person or persons unknown was returned.

Norman Rickard had been a civil servant working at the Admiralty. 264A Elgin Avenue was owned by a retired Civil Servant who was Norman Rickard's landlord. His landlord said that Norman Rickard had been living with him since the middle of 1961. He said:

I saw very little of him. But he was a good, quiet tenant who paid his rent regularly.

264A Elgin Avenue, Maida Vale

He said that on 14 February 1962 that a man called at the house from the Admiralty saying that Norman Rickard had not been into work and inquired as to whether he was ill. He said:

Mr Rickard's flat was locked, but we got in and looked around. There were no signs of disorder or upset.

However, he noted that there had been three days' supply of milk outside.

He said that a few days later a woman police constable called and looked around Norman Rickard's room, and then on the following Monday two women police constables arrived. The landlord said:

They said they were looking for certain personal articles of Mr Rickard's and said that if they were not there it would show he had gone away and taken them with him.

The landlord said that they searched through his drawers and suitcases and then thought that they had better look into the wardrobe to see if there were any papers in there. He said:

The wardrobe was locked but they opened it and I could see the body inside.

A man that had lived in Islingwood Place in Brighton said that during the afternoon of Saturday 10 February 1962 he saw Norman Rickard in Marble Arch. He said:

I recollect seeing him round Marble Arch on previous occasions, but on that afternoon I got into conversation with him in the Edgeware Road. We walked around and looked at the shops and then went to Foyle's bookshop where I believe he bought a book.

He went on to say that he left Norman Rickard at about 5.30pm and arranged to meet him later at Maida Vale station and that Norman Rickard agreed to meet him between 8pm and 8.15pm. However, he said that when Norman Rickard didn't turn up that he found his house and rang the bell of the flat but got no reply. He then said:

I went back to the station and waited a while and then went back again but there was still no reply.

However, he said that he then went back to the station and decided to wait a little longer in case he turned up and then saw him coming up the road with another man. He said that Norman Rickard saw him, but didn't speak to him as he passed with the other man, going in the direction of his flat.

He said that on both occasions Norman Rickard had been wearing a leather jacket, blue jeans and leather boots with high heels. He noted that the other man was dressed 'quite differently' with a dark raincoat and ordinary suit trousers showing beneath.

He noted that since Norman Rickard's body was found that he had attended identity parades but had not been able to identify anyone as the person he saw with Norman Rickard.

The man said:

It was pure accident that I met Rickard that afternoon, but if he had kept the appointment he would have been quite safe with me.

When he was questioned by the Coroner, he said that he did believe that Norman Rickard had been a homosexual.

A German domestic servant who gave evidence with the aid of an interpreter who had lived in Biddulph Mansions in Paddington said that Norman Rickard introduced himself to her at about 7pm on the Saturday evening in a Piccadilly restaurant. She said that he started chatting to her about the weather and that they then left the restaurant together and went for a walk, looking at shop windows and then both caught the same train and both got off at Maida Vale. She said that she then walked with him along Elgin Avenue, noting that he seemed very nervous and had looked around as if he thought there was someone following him.

She said that she had been wearing trousers on the evening concerned and that Norman Rickard had been wearing a tweed jacket and black shoes.

264A Elgin Avenue, Maida Vale

The pathologist that carried out the post mortem said that he had first examined Norman Rickard's body whilst it was still in the wardrobe. He said that his body had been upside down in the wardrobe with his head resting against some shoes and that he had been dead for some time. He said that a dressing gown cord was knotted around his neck and that there was a singlet acting as a gag in his mouth and his wrists were tied behind his back with electric flex. He said:

It would have been quite impossible for him to have tied himself in this way alone.

He gave his cause of death as strangulation, adding:

It seems that he died from asphyxia during some unnatural practice.

A police detective superintendent said that so far, the man that had seen Norman Rickard earlier in the day and waited for him at the station and the German woman had been unable to reconcile their ideas on what Norman Rickard had been wearing when they saw him. However, he noted that Norman Rickard must have been alive on the Sunday morning after the man and the woman had seen him on the Saturday. The police detective superintendent said:

For he posted a letter home to Plymouth on the Sunday morning in which he mentioned listening to the 1 o'clock news and the weather forecasts. He said in the letter that he was going to have lunch and go for a walk before the rain came on.

The detective added that they had found Norman Rickard's jewellery concealed in his flat as well as his wallet and said that his cases and a holdall were found padlocked. He said:

He had apparently gone out expecting to bring someone home with him.

Noting that it was understood that robbery was a common fear among homosexuals of Norman Rickard's type.

The detective said that since Norman Rickard's body had been found that 2,000 people had been interviewed and 400 statements taken, but said that they had been unable to unearth the person concerned.

When the Coroner summed up he said:

Clearly this man was indulging in unnatural practice with another and sometime during this practice he died.

It is clear that he had gone out to solicit because he had locked his valuables away.

Maida Vale Station

The Coroner went on to state that an unnatural practice involving violence was 'a regrettable but fairly standard perversion'. He said that tied up as he was, Norman Rickard was exposed to risked, but that it was up to the jury to decide whether his death merely occurred during the act or whether there had been any intention to do injury and rob him.

It was also noted at the inquest that the police were also treating the case of Alan John Vigar, who was murdered at 29 St Georges Drive, Pimlico on 19 February 1962, as being connected.

After hearing the evidence the jury returned a verdict of murder by person or persons unknown.

Lily Stephenson

Age: 61

Sex: female

Date: 31 Jan 1962

Place: Springfield Place, Barnsley

Lily Stephenson was found dead in an alleyway near her home at Springfield Place, Barnsley on 31 January 1962.

She had been raped and left to die about 100 yards from her home.

She was reported missing after she failed to return home from a shopping expedition on 30 January 1962.

Her death was given as being due to acute or chronic bronchitis, accelerated by shock, following and due to a fracture of the nose and upper jaw after a blow by a fist or some hard object.

Following the post mortem it was ascertained that an attempt had been made to commit buggery with her, and some degree of penetration had been achieved. In addition, a complete intercourse per vagina had been accomplished. There was no evidence of robbery. No weapon was found and the facial injuries she had sustained were consistent with her having been struck a violent blow by a clenched fist.

As such, it was reported that sexual assault appeared to have been the motive for the crime.

The Coroner said:

This woman was foully murdered.

It was heard that Lily Stephenson had been extremely ill and that her facial injuries would not have caused death in a healthy person. Additionally it was heard that her injuries suggested that she had been struck a blow that had rendered her unconscious or semi-conscious and that she had been raped.

The police said that they were considering whether the murder was connected to that of Mabel Metcalfe who was murdered 16 miles away in Dewsbury.

Shortly after she was found murdered, Scotland Yard were called in to carry out the investigation.

They appealed for anyone that had seen her after she left her home at 4.45pm on the Tuesday to go into town for her shopping to come forward.

The police appealed for information about a man who might have been seen in the vicinity of the murder on 30 January 1962. He was described as:

- About 30.
- Slim.
- 5ft 4in tall.
- Brown hair, brushed back and slightly bushy.

They also appealed for information about two men seen walking along Bodworth Road in Barnsley on the night of her murder. They said that the men had been eating from a paper bag containing either pies or sandwiches.

The police said they interviewed 3,000 people in connection with the murder as well as taking statements from 4,500 people and checking the movements of 2,155 workers in the district.

Her husband, a 68-year-old retired miner, said that Lily Stephenson had no enemies and had never complained of being molested. He said that every evening, except Thursday, she followed the same routine of visiting three shops in Dodsworth Road, Barnsley. He added that he could see no reason why she would go into the alleyway where she was found.

Lily Stephenson was noted as having been a club pianist and a former ENSA pianist.

Her inquest returned a verdict of murder by some person or persons unknown.

Bryan Jackson and Noel Mellors

Age: 31 and 19

Sex: male and male

Date: 24 Jan 1962

Place: Kneesall

Bryan Jackson and Noel Mellors died in a car crash.

The Vauxhall Velox car they were in had gone off the road at Kneesall on 24 January 1962 and demolished a telegraph pole.

An open verdict was returned, with the Coroner noting that the verdict implied at least some thread of negligence.

They had been rear seat passengers in a car driven by a 32-year-old man that lived in Charles Street, Newark.

The man appeared at the inquest, along with another man that had been in the car, both of them on crutches, but neither of them could remember anything about the accident.

A police constable that examined the car after the crash said that it appeared to have been properly serviced and that if driven properly, there was nothing to account for it suddenly leaving the road.

When the Coroner addressed the jury, he told them that it was on that evidence that they had to discharge their duty of returning a verdict. He added:

For lack of evidence or otherwise, there is nothing to justify your charging the driver with a serious offence. Did an accident happen? What did happen? Did a tyre burst? Did the driver momentarily doze? He can't remember himself, he was unconscious after the accident. Yet an open verdict by its nature must imply at least some thread of negligence.

The jury then returned an open verdict, owing to lack of evidence.

New Born Boy

Age: 0

Sex: male

Date: 23 Jan 1962

Place: Hampshire

The body of a newly born male child was found in Hampshire on 23 January 1962.

The death of the child was reported by the Hampshire Constabulary in their Homicide Return for 1962, Part II, but with no details beyond:

Although enquiries have been made into this matter, the current position is no different to that reported on the Part I of the Homicide Return.

Nothing more is known.

William Anthony Hamilton

Age: 26

Sex: male

Date: 22 Jan 1962

Place: 10 Downing Street, Westminster, London.

William Anthony Hamilton died whilst working on the rebuilding of 10 Downing Street in Westminster.

An open verdict was returned after his cause of death could not be determined.

He had lived in Stanlaka Road in Shepherd's Bush and had been a carpenter.

He collapsed at work just after clocking on and was taken to Westminster Hospital but was found to be dead on arrival.

His inquest heard that a most detailed examination of his body had been made but that nothing was revealed that could have caused his death. The only abnormality that could be found was that he had some inflammation in the bronchial tract, but there was no sign of pneumonia and it was not thought that he could have had a severe influenza infection because there was no evidence of that.

It was also heard that there was a story that something had fallen on his head some time before, but the post mortem found no abnormality whatsoever. The pathologist said that he could exclude any form of injury.

Following further examination, a pathologist said that he had been unable to find any satisfactory demonstrable cause of death. He said that examinations had been made to find a virus infection related to influenza, and that investigations had been made by Scotland Yard to trace poison, but they had proved negative.

He added that he was forced to the conclusion that his death, which usually fell into the 18 to 30 years of age group, had no demonstrable cause. He added that he had not seen one before in about 500 to 600 autopsies.

He added that he felt that his death must have been related to some abnormal pace-making of the heart. He said that there was no sign of injury whatever, but that hurrying to work to clock in might have precipitated his death.

William Hamilton's brother said that William Hamilton was married and had come to the United Kingdom from New Zealand in December 1960 and had intended to go back to New Zealand one day. He said that about three months earlier a hammer fell on his head and he was treated at St George's Hospital and had some stitches inserted, but didn't stop work.

A labourer who lived in Henshaw Street, Walworth, said that whilst waiting to be directed by a foreman to work at Downing Street on 22 January 1962, he saw William Hamilton clock in at the time office after which he saw him stiffen and fall backwards.

He said that a crowd then went to his aid.

He said that no one pushed or touched him prior to his falling and that it all happened very quickly.

He said that it was just about two minutes after 8am and that he thought that William Hamilton had been hurrying to clock in.

His inquest concluded that his cause of death was unascertainable and it was heard that the Coroner knew of only two such cases in 21,000 and that they happened in the 18 to 30 age group. The Coroner noted that there was no question that his death was anything other than natural, but that the difficulty was to give it a label. He said that it was a rarity, and recorded an open verdict.

10 Downing Street is noted for being the residence of the Prime Minister of England.

Joseph Maguire

Age: 2 months

Sex: male

Date: 17 Jan 1962

Place: Elgin Crescent, Notting Hill, London

Joseph Maguire died from haemorrhage due to a fractured skull on 17 January 1962.

He was found dead in his cot by his father at their home in Elgin Crescent, Notting Hill.

An open verdict was returned at his inquest.

He had been a twin and had been born by breach delivery in Queen charlotte's Hospital in Hammersmith on 16 November 1961.

His inquest heard that it was a mystery as to how he came by his injury and the Coroner said that there was insufficient evidence as to the circumstances of his death.

Joseph Maguire had had a twin sister who his father said was born quite normally. He added:

Joseph seemed to be extraordinarily quiet when he came home about two weeks after his birth. On January 17 my wife was preparing a bath for the twins and left Joseph in his cot. But when I picked him up he was just not moving. I took him to a doctor, who told me the baby was dead. To my knowledge he had not received a knock or a fall on the head.

Elgin Crescent, Notting Hill

His mother said that he couldn't recollect Joseph Maguire having knocked his head, but had noticed that he had been quiet and had 'cried pathetically'.

The doctor that attended the delivery of the twins said that the girl had been born normally, but that forceps had been used to deliver Joseph Maguire. She added:

I have heard that a fracture of the skull can be caused by forceps.

The doctor that carried out the post mortem said that Joseph Maguire died from a haemorrhage due to a fracture of the skull and that he thought the fracture had been a fresh one.

Edward Hunter

Age: 41

Sex: male

Date: 12 Jan 1962

Place: Harrow Weald

Edward Hunter was found dead in a stream near Cow Lane not far from the Thames.

He died from drowning, however, the stream was only 2ft 6in deep.

A police constable that went to the stream, said that he found no signs of violence or foul play.

The pathologist said that he had been dead for at least two weeks. He said that he found no traces of disease or bruising and that his cause of death had been drowning.

His father said that as far as he knew that is son had no reason to take his own life, adding:

When he came to visit us at Christmas he seemed perfectly happy and untroubled.

He had lived at 26 College Close in Harrow Yeald.

The Coroner said:

It is impossible to tell how he got into the stream.

Agnes Walsh

Age: 65

Sex: female

Date: 11 Jan 1962

Place: River Thames

Agnes Walsh was found dead in the River Thames.

River Thames

She was the sister of the governor of Wandsworth Prison, a Brigadier, who was also the chairman of Westminster's housing committee and who had previously been the governor of Lincoln Prison from 1947 to 1952.

She was found dead in the river 17 days after she went missing from her home in Morpeth Mansions, Victoria where she had lived with another woman.

Her inquest was held on 2 February 1962 where an open verdict was returned.

Agnes Walsh had been the warden of St Anne's Settlement at Vauxhall where she was said to have spent her life looking after the old and sick of a poor London parish. Her brother said that she had been suffering from a nervous breakdown.

John Brown

Age: 60

Sex: male

Date: 4 Jan 1962

Place: A706, West Lothian

John Brown was found dying from gunshot wounds on the A706 on 3 January 1962 and died the following day in hospital.

He had been shot in the head and body.

The murder took place on the side of the Lanarkshire to Whitburn Road (A706) between Wilsontown and Breich, about 500 yards north of the boundary between Lanarkshire and Midlothian.

A 21-year-old man, a miner, was tried but acquitted after a not proven verdict was returned.

John Brown had been a master butcher and farmer from Stirlingshire with a shop at Bunessan, Main Street in Buchlyvie.

It was reported that he had been driving along the ice-bound A706, over 1,000 feet up the Gladsmuir Hills between Forth and Wast Calder, when he was flagged down by three men standing beside a car. He stopped and was going to their assistance when he was shot at least three times.

It was said that he had been stopped at about 3pm by the three men. They were described as:

- Between 20 and 30.
- Medium build and height.
- Wearing light coloured short raincoats.

John Brown was later found injured and taken to Bangour Hospital where he underwent an emergency operation, but died on the morning of 4 January 1962. Before he died, he gave three or four statements about the men involved in the incident.

John Brown had not been on a journey that he made regularly and it was thought that he had been heading to Fauldhouse to visit a relative.

It had been snowing around the time and the moors and road were described as snow-covered.

It was initially thought that he might have been shot by a mad man and mental institutions were checked for escapees.

After shooting him the men drove off with his two-tone blue and white Triumph Herald car, registration SWG 600, which was later found abandoned eight miles away at Whitburn. It was noted that apart from taking his car, John Brown had not been robbed and nor had the car been searched before it was abandoned.

The murder was described as motiveless.

Five shotgun cartridges were found at the scene.

It was later reported that a car fitting the description of one used by the murderers had been previously seen parked at the scene of the crime with one man in it and another standing in the road. The man seen standing in the road was described as:

- Between 20 and 35.
- About 5ft 10in tall.
- Wearing a dark overcoat.

It was reported that shortly before John Brown was shot that another car was flagged down by the men, but it didn't stop.

The police said they were interested in tracing anyone who owned a 12-bore single-barrel repeating shotgun that held five cartridges along with anyone that had been in licenced premises near the scene and seen two or three men with either a gun or a car. The police noted that the gun used in the crime was not common.

They said:

We found five spent cartridges from it at the scene. Someone heard them being fired in quick succession at about 3.05pm, but we cannot estimate how many hit Mr Brown.

At the hospital, before his death, John Brown told his son that he had stopped to help some lads and that after having given them some assistance with their car, he was going back to his when they said it was a hold-up. After that he said:

The young ----- shot me.

The following morning after that John Brown underwent an emergency operation, but died at 9.35am.

Two men were initially arrested for his murder 36 hours after the crime, but one of them, a 24-year-old, was discharged on 5 March 1962 and gave evidence for the Crown. However, it was claimed that his evidence was unreliable and that in part, his testimony was given in order to ensure his release.

At the trial at the High Court in Edinburgh following a four-day trial a jury of nine men and six women, following a retirement of an hour and a half, returned a majority verdict of not proven. There were 82 witnesses in the case and 61 productions, including two shotguns.

About 50 members of the public had queued outside in Parliament Square to obtain entry to the public benches at the trial, which were described as being well filled by the time the jurors were called.

The court heard evidence from the other man that had said that he had seen the man fire the shots that killed John Brown. However, the judge noted that his evidence had to be taken with special care with the judge noting that however reliable his evidence:

There must be corroboration of that evidence from a separate and independent source.

It was heard that the other man had given evidence that if accepted, overthrew John Brown's own evidence, as well as that of two other witnesses at the trial and that as such, if he could not be believed then the man on trial had to be acquitted.

When the judge addressed the jury he said:

The witness could hardly be described as having played a very noble part in the proceedings. The Crown had to prove its case beyond reasonable doubt. If after hearing all the evidence, you are left in reasonable doubt as to whether the Crown has brought home guilt to the accused, it is your duty to give him the benefit of doubt and bring in a verdict of not guilty or not proven. But it has got to be a reasonable doubt, not just a spectre of doubt or an academic doubt.

The other man said that the accused man had spoken to him on several occasions about buying a gun and that he later bought a shotgun at Falkkirk, a five-shot repeater.

He said that on the day of the murder the accused man called on him in the forenoon and said that he had 30 cartridges and asked him to accompany him rabbit shooting in a field. He said that his car wouldn't start and the accused man put the weapon in the rear seat and helped to start it by pushing it. He said that they then drove off to Westerton via Breich cross roads and that when he tried to turn the car to return to Longridge that the engine started to splutter.

He said that whilst he worked under the bonnet that the accused man stopped another car, which then drove off and that the accused man told him that the driver had not had a spanner. However, he said that soon after a Triumph Herald drew up, the driver of which was John Brown, who offered the use of his tools.

After the shooting he said he panicked and drove off in his own car towards Breich crossroads and was overtaken along the way by the accused man driving the Triumph.

He said that he then ran out of petrol at Breich crossroads and whilst there was again passed by the accused man in the Triumph.

He said that after then refuelling he drove home to Longridge.

The driver of the first car that pulled up, a vehicle salesman, said that after attending Lanark Market on 3 January 1962, he was returning to Edinburgh and that just after crossing the Midlothian County boundary he saw a stationery car. He said:

As I approached the car a man stepped out from the front of it and waved me down. I stopped just past the stationery car. He came up to the door and asked if I could lend him a shifting spanner. I said I could not and had no other keys. Then another car came out of the fog and compelled me to go on. I only saw this man for about ten seconds. He was between 20 and 30.

He added that he felt that there had been another person present on the other side of the car.

He said that he later attended an identification parade at Saughton Prison eight days later but could not be sure of an identification. He said:

I looked at number two and another man. Number two seemed to be the most likely fellow who spoke to me, but his height seemed to be shorter than I remembered. I spoke to another man who was taller and then I asked each of them to say, 'Will you give me a shifting spanner'. I could not be sure. Number two was the likeliest but I could not be sure.

A number of other people saw the car on the side of the road including a 36-year-old dairymaid from Rusha Farm, a 57-year-old lorry driver from Polbeth and a 26-year-old driver's mate from Braehead. The diver's mate said that one of the man had been wearing a 'Robin Hood' hat, a soft white coloured hat with a dark feather.

They were also seen by a 53-year-old coal merchant from Braehead and a 26-year-old miner from Wester Green Wall Farm.

The 26-year-old miner said that he had passed the county boundary at about 3pm and saw two cars, one a green car and the other a Triumph Herald. He said they were about a yard or two apart and that the boot of the Triumph Herald had been open and the bonnet of the green car was up. He said that he also saw a man standing at the open bonnet of the green car and another man walking from the Triumph Herald to the green car.

The judge said that there were two chapters in the case, stating that the first was:

Is it proved beyond reasonable doubt that the victim met his death by shooting and secondly, if so, is the Crown case proved beyond reasonable doubt that it was the accused who was the perpetrator?

It was added that the real problem in the case was whether it had been proved beyond reasonable doubt that it had been the accused man that had done the shooting.

It was noted that the Crown case started with the other man, whose evidence it was stated had to be taken with consideration, in particular with the fact that up until a month earlier he had himself been included in the murder charge. The judge said:

Here is a man, who was arrested and charged with the crimes that accused was charged with. It was not until the beginning of the month that the charge was dropped and he was released. It is perfectly true that now that he has given evidence he can no longer be proceeded against on this charge. But, he has an interest, or he will have an interest, to minimise the part which he played, and to throw the blame on the accused.

As such, the judge noted that his evidence had to be treated with special care and that if it was rejected, then the man on trial had to be acquitted, noting that his evidence went against that given by the murdered man himself, John Brown.

The man on trial used a defence of alibi, saying that he was at home at the time. His special defence read:

On the afternoon of January 3, from about 2.15pm he was walking along the main road from Longridge to his home at 3 Union Road, Whitburn, and was thereafter in his home until about 3.40pm between which times the alleged crime is believed to have been committed.

His father and brother gave evidence to say that they had come into the house at 3.30pm to find the man there and some soup boiling.

The defence submitted that the man would not have been able to drive from the scene of the crime, at 2.55pm to 3.05pm to Redmill, a journey of 13 minutes, and to have then walked the 1.6 miles from Redmill Cottages to his own home and to have been there with soup on the boil at 3.30pm.

However, the prosecution stated that by their calculations the man could have been back at home by 3.20pm after having shot John Brown.

It was heard that John Brown had left Lanark sometime after 2.30pm, or at the worst for the defence at 2.35pm, on a journey in appalling conditions, which had taken everyone else who made it that day 25 to 30 minutes. As such, it was said that John Brown could not have been at the locus of the shooting before the earliest of 2.55pm. It was further submitted that the shooting must have occurred closer to 3pm and that in fact a witness heard the five shots fired at what they claimed to be 3.05pm.

The witness that heard the shots had been a 45-year-old miner from Forth that had been out shooting foxes on the moors on the east side of the Firth-West Calder road. He said that he heard five shots from the north, which was the direction of the road and that they were all fired within half a minute. He said:

I thought it was a repeater shot gun.

He said that he gave up then for the day as he thought that the shooting would have disturbed any foxes that might have been about. He estimated that he heard the shots at 3pm or shortly afterwards.

John Brown was discovered by a 27-year-old joiner from Longridge lying on the side of the road. He said that he drove past two vehicles first, the leading one which looked like a Triumph Herald and the other like a green van or car after which he saw a man lying at the side of the road. He said that he actually passed him before he realised it was a man and that he then went back with a lorry driver and found John Brown lying face down and parallel with the verge and a good deal of blood. He said that he then drove to Forth to fetch help and then returned and when he returned he saw three cartridges in the road lying near the man's cap.

During their investigation the police drove the route from the shooting to Redhill and timed it at 13 minutes. They further stated that it would have taken the man 20 to 25 minutes to have walked the 1.6 miles from Redhill to his house, which in total meant that the whole journey would have taken him 33 to 38 minutes, meaning that if the shooting had taken place at 3pm, he would not have arrived home until 3.33pm to 3.38pm.

However, it was conceded that two witnesses had seen the man on trial in the outskirts of Whitburn at about 3.15pm on the day of the shooting and that he was thought to have arrived at 3.07pm. The man had lived at 3 Union Road in Whitburn.

In his evidence the man on trial had said that he had got out of the other man's car at the crossroads and gone home and fiddled about in his house and made soup, etc. The defence noted that if his alibi had been a lie that he could thought up a better one, or even said that he had been with the other man at the time of the shooting and that it had been the other man that had pulled the trigger.

However, it was noted that he had said, that after the murder, he had later gone out in his car and that one of two places he visited was the scene of the crime, which the judge noted:

You may think that is significant.

It was also noted that when the accused man was cautioned and charged with the theft of the car, he said:

Sorry about the whole thing now. You will get the gun in the cemetery.

However, it was noted that in his statements he had said that he had last seen the gun about 2.30pm when the other man left to go to Fauldhouse with it. As such, it was asked how he could have known that the gun had been in the cemetery. It was however noted that he had later said that the other man had told him that the gun, after having been used, had been mutilated and left in the cemetery. The judge commented:

Do you see how necessary it was for the accused to explain away how he came to know about the gun when he told police about it. There are many other points of a similar kind in this case.

It was further stated that when he had said he was sorry, that he claimed that he was sorry for not having told the police about the gun sooner. However, it was submitted that the key that broke down that explanation was the adjective 'whole', noting that that was his answer to the charge at the time, but that it was the murder that he had been thinking about.

The defence stated however, that what he had been saying that he was that he was sorry that he had known that the gun was in the bush and that the other man had had it on the afternoon of 3 January 1962 and that he had done nothing about it. The defence noted that if he had said, 'Yes, I did it, I am sorry about the whole thing now', that it would have been a different matter, but that he didn't say anything like that, and just that he was sorry that he hadn't gone to the police earlier.

It was further noted that regardless of his alibi, there were no corroborative witnesses until 3.30pm when his relatives returned.

When the accused man took the stand, he repeatedly denied having had any involvement in the murder.

He said that he first heard of the murder on TV at 6pm on the day it occurred.

It was reported that there was also a dramatic scene when the accused man left the witness-box and donned a fawn-coloured raincoat and demonstrated with a shotgun for the benefit of the jury.

Regarding the gun, he said that his friend told him that it had been 'cut off' and that he had left it at the Old Cemetery in a bush. The gun was later found in the bush at the cemetery at South Whitburn Church. Another part of the gun, the barrel, was found in a stream, White Burn, in Whitburn by a footbridge by a civil engineer equipped with a mine detecting device.

The gun had been a Savage 12-bore repeater shotgun of American manufacture. About 15 inches of the barrel had been sawn off and the butt had also been sawn off about 4 inches behind the grip. A senior lecturer in forensic medicine at Edinburgh University was given the gun parts and said that they all fitted together and were parts of the same gun.

The senior lecturer also examined John Brown's clothing, including a brown overcoat that had three ragged holes in the left chest, left shoulder and in the back and went on to say that following tests he determined that John Brown had been shot from a range of 2 yards to 3½ yards.

A 27-year-old oncost worker at Polkemmet Colliery, who lived in Longridge said that on the afternoon of 30 December 1961 that he saw the accused man with a repeater shotgun which he was admiring. He said that whilst they were at a farm the accused man told him that he had bought the gun and that he had always had a notion for a gun. He added that the accused man also had a packet of cartridges.

The 27-year-old oncost worker added that he saw the accused man and the other man involved on 3 January 1962 leave the other man's house and walk towards a car which he said they had difficulty starting. He noted that he saw no gun on that occasion.

Another loose end described a the trial was the time of the shooting. It was submitted that a sort of anchor in the matter of time was the fact that the other man had been seen by three witnesses at the Breich crossroads just two miles to the north of the spot where John Brown was shot, having at that time run out of petrol and having had an empty tin filled up by the petrol attendant at the crossroads. The petrol attendant said that the man had come into her filling station at just about 3pm. The time was also corroborated by three men that the man gave a lift to along with another man that came out of a public house there at 3pm.

With regard to the accused man, it was noted that he had been driving a 'hot car' and that he had arrived in Redmill at about 3.07pm and was seen just after that walking along the pavement by a couple from their car.

It was claimed that the evidence fitted him like a glove, that being the distance of 1½ miles from the place where the car was abandoned at 3.07pm, and him having walked half a mile to the point where he was seen at 3.15pm by the couple, meaning that he would have reached home by about 3.20pm.

However, it was noted that the accused man denied that the person the couple had seen at 3.15pm had been him.

Regarding the issue of a motive, it was said:

It is clear that whoever did this crime does not seem to have had a motive. Brown was not robbed, the Herald, although technically stolen, was just used to make a getaway. There is no suggestion in the case that anyone had a motive.

It was also noted that the accused man's house in Union Street was close to the cemetery where the gun was found, whilst the other man, who he claimed had told him he had put it there, had lived 1¾ miles away at 49 Northfield Crescent in Longridge. The prosecution said:

You may think it is a rather strange arm of coincidence that of all the places in West Lothian or in Scotland where the sawn-up gun is found, it is found in a yew tree but a step from the accused man's house.

The defence noted that the gun however, was in the one bush at the cemetery where it shouldn't have been hidden, that being the one near the church gate and in the light, noting that if the accused man had hidden it he would have done so elsewhere and that the guns position suggested that it had been hidden there by a person not well acquainted with the area.

It was further heard that the accused man said that he had gone to look at the gun and after pulling it out, that he had put it back, but with the butt of the gun showing. It was said that if he had have been the murderer then he would not have left the butt of the gun showing.

It was also noted that the police searched his home and not a trace of the gun having been sawn up there was found on his hacksaw, or clothing or elsewhere.

The prosecution stated that they had built up a circumstantial case against the accused man, without the evidence of the other man, but that if they added the evidence of the other man then you had an actual eye witness to the murder.

When the defence addressed the jury, they submitted that it was enough for the jury to say to themselves that the other man may be lying and that if he was, then the accused man might be innocent.

The accused man was said to have received the verdict of not proven without emotion and to have then left the court through a side door without looking at the jury as he did so.

It was reported on Sunday 15 April 1962 that the gun used would not be returned to the accused man. A spokesman for the Crown Office in Edinburgh, said:

Although the accused man was cleared of the murder, the police will not be returning the gun to him. Weapons used in murder are never returned. It might be put up for sale or retained for lecture purposes.

John McNally

Age: 72

Sex: male

Date: 3 Jan 1962

Place: Shaftoe Street, North Shields

John McNally was found injured in Shaftoe Street and died seven weeks later.

He first said that he had simply collapsed, but later said he was hit by a car.

He had a broken arm, broken leg and face injuries.

Doctors said that it was unlikely that his injuries were caused by a simple collapse. However, the police said that they could find no trace of an accident.

He had told an ambulance driver that he had just collapsed and had not been knocked down. However, three weeks later he claimed that he had been knocked down by a car that didn't stop. He had been unable to give any description of the car.

He had lived in Savoury Road, Rosehill in Wallsend.

An open verdict was returned.

Printed in Great Britain
by Amazon